Cambridge Elements ☰

Elements in Political Psychology
edited by
Yanna Krupnikov
Stony Brook University

ISSUE PUBLICS

How Electoral Constituencies Hide in Plain Sight

Timothy J. Ryan
The University of North Carolina at Chapel Hill
J Andrew Ehlinger
The University of North Carolina at Chapel Hill

Shaftesbury Road, Cambridge CB2 8EA, United Kingdom

One Liberty Plaza, 20th Floor, New York, NY 10006, USA

477 Williamstown Road, Port Melbourne, VIC 3207, Australia

314–321, 3rd Floor, Plot 3, Splendor Forum, Jasola District Centre,
New Delhi – 110025, India

103 Penang Road, #05–06/07, Visioncrest Commercial, Singapore 238467

Cambridge University Press is part of Cambridge University Press & Assessment,
a department of the University of Cambridge.

We share the University's mission to contribute to society through the pursuit of
education, learning and research at the highest international levels of excellence.

www.cambridge.org
Information on this title: www.cambridge.org/9781009242417

DOI: 10.1017/9781009242400

First published 2023

A catalogue record for this publication is available from the British Library.

ISBN 978-1-009-24241-7 Paperback
ISSN 2633-3554 (online)
ISSN 2633-3546 (print)

Cambridge University Press & Assessment has no responsibility for the persistence
or accuracy of URLs for external or third-party internet websites referred to in this
publication and does not guarantee that any content on such websites is, or will
remain, accurate or appropriate.

Issue Publics: How Electoral Constituencies Hide in Plain Sight

Elements in Political Psychology

DOI: 10.1017/9781009242400
First published online: April 2023

Timothy J. Ryan
The University of North Carolina at Chapel Hill

J Andrew Ehlinger
The University of North Carolina at Chapel Hill

Author for correspondence: Timothy J. Ryan, tjr@email.unc.edu

Abstract: An often-forgotten passage of Philip Converse's classic essay on mass belief systems introduced the concept of an issue public – a segment of voters that has crystallized attitudes about a particular topic. Some people deeply care about particular topics, and they might be equipped to reach judgments on these topics. This simple idea could provide an important corrective to work that casts citizens' political competence in a negative light. But, previous attempts to evaluate the issue publics hypothesis have been unsatisfying. This Element proposes and tests a new measurement approach for identifying issue publics. The evidence gathered leads to the conclusion that issue publics exist, but are smaller and more particularistic than existing scholarship presumes them to be. As such, researchers underappreciate the significance of issue opinions in electoral politics.

Keywords: issue publics, public opinion, political psychology, interest groups, issue voting

ISBNs: 9781009242417 (PB), 9781009242400 (OC)
ISSNs: 2633-3554 (online), 2633-3546 (print)

Contents

"[t]here isn't one voter in 20,000 who knows my voting record ... except on the one thing that affects him."
—*Anonymous congressman interviewed by Richard Fenno (1978, 142).*

1 Eldon Gould's Particular Problem

In several respects, Eldon Gould is the caricature of a Republican voter. He is seventy-six years old, white, and lives in rural Illinois. He is a farmer – just like his father, grandfather, and son. He owns 500 acres of land, which he uses to grow corn and soybeans, and to raise hogs. The area where he lives is sparsely populated. In 2016, there were 898 registered voters spread over the thirty square miles his voting precinct encompasses – just about thirty people per square mile. In 2016, 73 percent of these individuals voted, and they supported Donald Trump over Hillary Clinton by a more than two-to-one ratio.[1] For his part, Gould says he was "a little surprised" when Donald Trump won the Republican presidential nomination in 2016. But in the same breath, he acknowledges, "I don't think there was any doubt in my mind that I would vote for him" (Barbaro 2018). And he did (Kitroeff 2019).

Gould does remember harboring some concerns about what Donald Trump had to say about trade during his presidential campaign. In a stark departure from Republican Party orthodoxy of the time, Trump was loudly critical of free trade arrangements. He called the North American Free Trade Agreement the "worst trade deal ... in the history of this country" (Barbaro 2018). He promised to discard the Trans-Pacific Partnership, a landmark trade deal between the United States and eleven other nations tentatively negotiated by the Obama administration. And he repeatedly bemoaned the trade deficit between the United States and its trading partners – especially China – suggesting that the United States' purchasing more goods from China than vice versa was a sign of an exploitive relationship.

It is easy to see why all this would make Gould uneasy. Gould estimates that 90 percent of the soy he grows is exported – substantially to China.[2] If the United States were to impose new taxes on Chinese imports, as Trump threatened to do, China would likely respond by taxing the goods it imports from the United States. The effects on Gould's bottom line could be drastic. And once a trade war began, it could be difficult to deescalate. If it were to go on long enough, it might even create an opening for South American countries – Brazil and Argentina are major soy producers – to displace the Sino-American trade relationship permanently.

---

[1] Election results retrieved from the Kane County Clerk's website at www.kanecountyclerk.org/ Elections/Pages/Election-Results-Archive.aspx.
[2] Approximately half of US soybean exports go to China (Davey & Cohen 2018).

Gould's concerns proved well-founded. In March of 2018, President Trump announced new tariffs on imported steel and aluminum. The ostensible rationale was national security: the administration argued that reliance on foreign metal imports degraded the American manufacturing base. However, given Trump's campaign promises and concurrent griping about "decades of unfair trade" (quoted in Swanson 2018), it was hard to take this rationale as anything other than a legal pretext. From there, things unfolded as Gould feared. In April, China retaliated with tariffs on 128 American exports – soybeans chief among them. Further tariffs were unrolled throughout 2018 in tit-for-tat fashion.

Trump's trade bouts received ample media coverage in outlets like the *New York Times*, but it is hard to know how much the typical American voter's opinions were really affected by them. There were a lot of other things going on. Major political headline-grabbers included Special Counsel Robert Mueller's investigation into 2016 election interference; the Trump administration's effort to obstruct that inquiry; a declared national emergency instated to redirect federal funds toward funding a border wall; a scandal involving the Trump administration's family separation policy for children of recent undocumented immigrants; the decision to withdraw from a nuclear arms pact with Iran; Supreme Court nomination hearings in which Christine Blasey Ford accused Brett Kavanaugh of sexual assault; and more. Stories about tariffs probably would not crack most individuals' top ten list of significant political events of 2018.

For farmers like Gould, however, the ups and downs of trade policy were impossible to ignore. In the months after China's soy tariffs took effect, the price of soybeans dropped to the lowest level in a decade (Hirtzer 2019), leading farmers to sell at a loss, or place their crops in storage in the hopes that prices would rebound. Meanwhile, China shifted most of its soy purchasing to Brazil. During negotiations in December 2018, China and the United States agreed to a ninety-day moratorium on fresh tariffs, sparking some hope of a thaw. But these negotiations failed, and in May 2019, Trump escalated the dispute with fresh tariffs on $200 billion of Chinese imports.

Few Americans followed all of these turns, but each was exhaustively covered in what Gould refers to as the "Ag Media." The Ag Media includes periodicals such as *AgriNews*, *Farm and Dairy*, and *Farm Journal*, and also syndicated daily shows on television (*AgDay*) and radio (*My Farm Radio*, *AgriTalk*). At agweb.com, an interested party can sign up for several dozen regular newsletters, such as *Drovers Daily* – "the latest cattle industry news and features delivered daily to keep you informed of industry issues." The produce-oriented newsletter, *The Packer*, has both AM and PM editions, as well as separate specialized editions focused on produce technology, organic produce, and produce retail trends. Professional organizations generate a stream of relevant press releases and other updates. The Iowa Soybean Association, for instance, has a regular podcast (*The State of Soy*). In addition, farmers can easily track prices and news on their smartphones with specialized apps such as "Farm Futures Mobile" and "Agrarian Mobile Information Center." Farmers have ample opportunities to follow relevant political events that others might miss.

Did the Trump administration's moves on trade policy influence Trump's support within the farm community? There are signs that it did. A *Farm Journal* poll found that, whereas more than 70 percent of farmers supported Trump in 2016, only 54 percent said they intended to vote for him as of August 2018.[3] More conclusively, statistical analysis of county-level voting patterns during the trade war found that soy production of 10,000 bushels in a county was associated with an 11 percentage point swing against the Republican Party between the 2016 and 2018 federal elections (above and beyond national trends during this time) (Chyzh & Urbatsch 2021). Perhaps to curb the political fallout, the Trump administration unrolled substantial bailout packages to offset farmer's losses – $12 billion in direct payments in 2018, and $14.5 billion in 2019 (Daniels & Wilkie 2019).

By 2020, the trade war had cooled and soybean prices had rebounded somewhat. Still, Joe Biden improved on Hillary Clinton's vote total in Gould's precinct by nearly 9 percentage points (38.49 percent for Biden compared to 29.89 percent for Clinton).[4]

Issue Publics

Walter Lippman, the early-twentieth-century journalist and political commentator, was no fan of direct democracy. His writings reflect an abiding skepticism that citizens could acquire – much less comprehend – the information that they needed to play more than a side role in politics. He opens *The Phantom Public*, one of his classic indictments of populism, as follows:

> The private citizen today has come to feel rather like a deaf spectator in the back row, who ought to keep his mind on the mystery off there, but cannot quite manage to keep awake. He knows he is somehow affected by what is going on. Rules and regulations continually, taxes annually, and wars occasionally remind him he is being swept along by great drifts of circumstances.

---

[3] The *Farm Journal* poll – the Farm Journal Pulse – is based on an opt-in panel of approximately 5,000 farmers who receive two poll questions via text message each month. Its reporting practices are not up to scientific standards – methodological details are elusive – but the fact that it is a long-running panel provides some assurance that over-time trends are not purely driven by selection effects.

[4] Election results retrieved from the Kane County Clerk's website at www.kanecountyclerk.org/Elections/Pages/Election-Results-Archive.aspx.

> Yet these public affairs are in no convincing way his affairs. They are for the most part invisible. They are managed, if they are managed at all, at distant centers, from behind the scenes, by unnamed powers. As a private person he does not know for certain what is going on, or who is doing it, or where he is being carried. No newspaper reports his environment so that he can grasp it; no school has taught him how to imagine it; his ideals, often, do not fit with it; listening to speeches, uttering opinions and voting do not, he finds, enable him to govern it. He lives in a world which he cannot see, does not understand, and is unable to direct. (Lippman 1925, 3–4)[5]

Indeed, politics often feels as though it exists only off in some distant place. A person might have a general sense of the major goings on – the things that garnered top headlines or which were fodder for commentary on social media. But their knowledge of the particulars is shallow, and understanding of their significance dim. As we discuss in Section 2, this is the consensus picture of citizen political engagement that has developed over several decades of public opinion research.

But sometimes, you cannot escape politics; it walks up and conks you on the head. Contrast Lippman's description above with the experience of Shane Goplin, a soybean farmer in central Wisconsin. Interviewed as the Trump administration was involved in trade negotiations with China, Goplin recounts that when Trump announced (via Twitter) that he intended to impose additional tariffs on Chinese goods, the price of soy promptly fell by ten cents per bushel – a shift with enormous ramifications for Goplin's crop revenue. "It was a $40,000 tweet," he remarked to the *New York Times* (quoted in Cohen 2019). Such an obvious cause-and-effect relationship stands in stark contrast to Lippman's image of politics. No behind-the-scenes dealing. No ambiguity about who acted and with what consequence. Just the matter of deciding the consequences.

Our aim in the pages that follow is to improve understanding of how political behavior is influenced by situations when politics takes on heightened personal significance – wherein a person or constituency has particular motivation to attend to developments in a particular area. We focus on these instances for two reasons.

First, these are instances that are likely to matter. As we elaborate in Section 2, political judgments, such as about candidates, are difficult to move. People have little factual knowledge about politics, pay sporadic attention to the news, have standing group loyalties, and as Lippman notes, have limited faculties with which to comprehend public policy developments, even if they knew what these were. Perhaps because they lack a psychological framework

---

[5] We wish we were well versed in the political commentary of the 1920s, but we discovered the quoted passage via Kinder & Kalmoe (2017, 2).

from which to arrive at reasoned judgments, they tend to follow cues from elites about what they should think when it comes various issues and events. Scenarios wherein people really care about a particular topic might represent an important departure from this default – the rare but critical instance in which people think for themselves, and political actors have a genuine opportunity to ply people away from their political habits and predispositions.

Second, the social scientific understanding of the politics of personal significance is underdeveloped. Political science does not have a consensus about such important questions as: How many political topics does a typical person care about? How many distinct topics are cared about in the electorate as a whole? What factors induce a person to care about a particular political topic? When a person cares about a topic, what are the consequences for attitude stability, persuadability, and judgments about candidates? As we elaborate in Section 2, while some of these questions have been addressed to some extent by previous work, they are rarely if ever considered as an interrelated whole.

The theoretical framework we use to unify these questions is that of *issue publics*. This phrase was coined by Phillip Converse in a classic study of citizen political sophistication to capture the notion that, while political unsophistication might be a sort of default condition, any particular political topic might have its own constituency that is more psychologically invested. Converse provided a convenient label, but several other early public opinion researchers independently arrived at an assessment that the basic idea was indispensable. Surprisingly, as we discuss in Section 2, the concept of issue publics never took hold – at least not to the extent it might have. We ask why not, and examine whether issues publics – considered anew – might shed new light on issue politics in the United States.

Our primary contributions focus on measurement. We demonstrate just how difficult it is to use survey-based tools to assess how many issue publics exist and to classify people as belonging to an issue public. As we elaborate in Section 3, the difficulty is that survey researchers, faced with a recurrent pressure to keep survey instruments short, tend to limit their examination of issue publics to a fairly small number of issues – commonly those that are in the public eye at a given moment. This tendency is understandable, but it is at odds with the theoretical conception of an issue public – particularly the notion that issue public members would attend to their personally important issue even when it is *not* in the public eye. In Section 3, we show that the standing approaches to identifying issue public members are likely afflicted with substantial measurement error, the aggregate effect of which is to lead scholars to underestimate the significance of issue voting.

In Section 4, we ask what a survey-based issue public measure would look like, if it were designed from the ground up. After all, many of the standing measures reviewed in Section 3 were written with some other purpose in mind, or were designed with constraints that do not apply to modern survey research. We propose a measurement approach that focuses on how respondents answer an open-ended question. The main advantage of this approach is that, rather than limiting the focus to a manageable number of issues, it allows issue publics to emerge organically from the associations our question prompt activates in respondents' minds. We test our measurement approach in two panel studies: one conducted on a convenience sample, and one on a large national sample. The approach is not perfect, but we find evidence that it reveals a face of issue public membership that other approaches do not: citizens attend to a much wider array of issues than past work suggests, and for many people, these issue-based connections endure over time.

In Section 5, we submit our measure to a more difficult test by assessing its ability to predict a quintessential political judgment: deciding for whom to vote. We develop a new experimental tool – what we refer to as a "bespoke" conjoint experiment – that examines how candidate stances on political issues influence citizens' votes. We surmount a long-standing challenge in issue public research: designing a procedure that allows respondents to belong to a vast array of different issue publics. When we do, we find that issue public voting is important. Our study participants' votes were influenced by candidate stances on issue public issues even more than by stances on the most salient issues on the national stage.

Thus, where public opinion research has, for decades, downplayed the significance of issue-based voting, we suggest that it exists to an underappreciated degree – masked by the considerable impediments to determining what issues citizens care about. We close the Element by discussing the implications of this result for survey practices, as well as the theoretical understanding of issue-based voting in the United States.

2 A Hostile Landscape for Issue Voting

Americans are routinely consulted about their opinions on political issues of the day. With some time spent on the website of the Gallup organization, for instance, one can find a wealth of high-quality polling data assessing Americans' policy views concerning abortion, crime, the environment, gun control, health care, immigration, gay rights, marijuana policy, taxes, and many other topics. The results of polls like these are popular fodder for discussion by journalists and pundits. What do Americans want their government to do? How are they reacting to the latest current events? How has American culture evolved over time?

Politicians are part of the polling ecosystem, too. Journalists commonly seek politicians' reaction to polling results that cut against their policy positions, such as when, in the days after a horrific school shooting in Uvalde, Texas, *Fox News Sunday* host Shannon Bream asked Republican Senator Mike Lee to react to polling data showing that upward of 75 percent of Americans favored several new restrictions of guns (Shapero 2022). And of course many candidates for office hire polling firms to collect proprietary data that will inform campaign activities.

However, the relationship between a particular poll result and the proper response by a public figure is anything but straightforward. The reason is that a summary poll result characterizing a constituency's position on a particular political topic might elide a lot of important context. For instance, suppose that a candidate for Congress is considering coming out in favor of marijuana decriminalization, but learns that 60 percent of her constituencies oppose this policy. Although that result might give the representative pause, there is a lot more she would want to think about. How many constituents *care* about marijuana policy? How does it stack up against other things that they might consider when casting a vote? What proportion of voters care enough about marijuana that they would donate money or attend a rally to advocate for their view? What proportion would change their mind if the policy were enacted and drug use did not seem to increase? How likely is a future political opponent to make marijuana policy a campaign issue? Our hypothetical candidate is struggling with an old question in political science: How much do political leaders need to attend and respond to citizens' issue opinions?

A more general statement of this point is that there is a gap – potentially a large one – between *views registered on surveys* and *public opinion*, which in V. O. Key's memorable definition is "opinions held by private persons which governments find it prudent to heed" (1961, 14). Surveys summarize the views of a cross section of individuals at one moment in time, in dimensions specified by the person conducting the survey. Public opinion, in contrast, is embedded in a complex political system in which the openings for citizen involvement are multifarious – elections, but also activism, donations, discourse, and persuasion – and some opinions have greater potential to animate than others.

When the canonical approaches to survey research – probability sampling and a standardized questionnaire – were invented in the mid-twentieth century, social scientists promptly criticized them for treating all opinions as equally important and efficacious. In a biting critique presented to the *American Sociological Society*, Herbert Blumer argued that the then young enterprise of public opinion polling was premised on a *nonsequitur:* polls could predict elections well enough, but elections are an aberration from typical channels for political influence. Most political influence occurs via pressure points – individuals or groups influencing key figures (committees, boards, legislators, administrators, bureaucrats, and so forth), and "these key individuals take into account what they judge to be worthy of being taken into account" (Blumer 1948, 544). These people were probably only passingly interested in an amalgamation of atomized opinions lumped together into proportions or averages – what public opinion polls deliver. Much more, they would care about individuals' or groups' capacity to sustain attention, to elicit messaging from the opposition party, to mobilize, to secure meetings, and to persuade. Blumer exhorted social scientists to embed their examination of opinions in the public in a more explicit theory of which opinions matter and why (Blumer 1948).[6]

Consider also V. O. Key's classic discussion of the role of public opinion within democracy, which we allude to above. Which opinions would politicians find it "prudent to heed?" For Key, the answer depended, yes, on how many people held each opinion – but also on the intensity with which they were held. Key writes:

> Obviously the incidence of opinion intensity within the electorate about an issue or problem is of basic importance for politics. An issue that arouses only opinion of low intensity may receive only the slightest attention, while one that stirs opinions of high intensity among even relatively small numbers of people may be placed high on the governmental agenda. (14)

In his analysis, Key elucidates that the distribution of attitude intensity would have major implications for how many citizens became aware of a political controversy, and who would be more likely to effectively wield influence. "Under proper circumstances extremely small numbers of persons can generate sufficient uproar to make life miserable for those in power. They may make themselves distinctly heard as they seek to obtain or, perhaps more commonly, to obstruct action" (Key 1961, 92).

Philip Converse, a key figure in the earliest survey-based work on public opinion, also recognized the importance of understanding citizens' psychological investment in particular political issues. His most famous essay, "The Nature of Belief Systems in Mass Publics," is most commonly remembered for elucidating Americans' political naiveté: their attitudes about particular issues did not hang together in an ideologically coherent way; their political views shifted erratically over time; and for most, their comprehension of words like "liberal" and "conservative" was flimsy at best. But in a less-cited passage near the end of the essay, Converse carves out an important caveat: even if

---

[6] See Converse (1987) for a thoughtful retrospective on Blumer's critique.

Americans' political sophistication is *generally* low, they might pay attention to topics of particular personal significance.

> The simple conclusion seems to be that different controversies excite differ-
> ent people to the point of real opinion formation. One man takes an interest in
> policies bearing on the Negro and is relatively indifferent to or ignorant about
> controversies in other areas. His neighbor may have few crystallized opinions
> on the race issue, but he may find the subject of foreign aid very important.
> Such sharp divisions of interest are part of what the term "issue public" is
> intended to convey. (Converse 1964, 246)

Converse closes by alluding to some results that roughly support this notion, though he clearly thought the data available to him in 1964 were mostly insufficient to the task.

In the early days of survey-based public opinion research, then, there was substantial recognition that understanding the causes and consequences of citizens becoming psychologically invested in particular political issues was essential for contextualizing survey results, and understanding what role political attitudes play in a dynamic political system.

Two Trajectories of Research on Issue Publics

How have political scientists come to understand the role of issues publics since these initial discussions? The answer is: unevenly. In our reading, there is a substantial rift between literatures on public policy and political institutions, where issue publics are a focal concept, and public opinion, where the concept is surprisingly elusive.

First, consider the research that focuses on public policy and political institutions. Here, issue publics, also known as interest groups, are a canonical topic – the focus of a chapter in almost every introductory textbook on American politics. Well-regarded books document how issues influence candidates on the campaign trail (Fenno 1978 [see our epigraph]; Sulkin 2005). There is also evidence that they exert substantial influence on policy outcomes. Interest groups form to advocate for a wide spectrum of causes: workers' rights, environmental issues, changes to social policy, senior citizens' interests, interests of particular industry sectors, and more. They use many tactics to advance their goals, several of which rely on participation from large numbers of regular citizens: letter-writing campaigns, social media campaigns, organized protests, get-out-the-vote campaigns, posting flyers and lawn signs, making campaign contributions, and so forth (Kollman 1998). These efforts appear to influence policy makers, either via persuasion (Austen-Smith 1996) or by improving the return that policy makers receive for exerting effort in a particular policy area (Hall & Deardorff 2006).

Perhaps the most commonly invoked example of the influence that interest groups can wield concerns gun control. Since at least the early 1990s, the American public as a whole has reliably supported stricter gun laws. In a Gallup survey as of March 2018, for instance, 67 percent of Americans wanted stricter gun control laws, compared to 4 percent who wanted less-strict laws and 28 percent who favored the laws being "kept as they are" (Jones 2018). Of course, you wouldn't know it by looking at public policy. In the past several years, a series of mass shootings in the United States induced repeated calls for new federal restrictions: tighter background checks for gun purchases, a ban on assault-style weapons, a ban on large-capacity magazines, and so forth. Over and over again, these initiatives failed.[7] To be sure, part of the reason for the failure is the insider influence of the gun lobby. But at least as important is the NRA's success in forming a collection of regular citizens who pay attention to gun policy, write letters to representatives, donate money to political groups, and vote – particularly in primary elections – on the basis of gun issues, thereby constraining the behavior of political actors (Lacombe 2019).

Given the centrality of interest groups as a political science concept, as well as the initial interest in incorporating issue publics into the study of mass political behavior, one might expect public opinion researchers to have proceeded in parallel. For instance, public opinion researchers might have developed a common understanding of how to determine citizens' issue public memberships. They might have documented how many issue publics exist, the extent to which they overlap, how many issue publics a typical person belongs to, and many other things. In fact, these efforts have occurred on a small scale, or not at all. On the contrary, the trend in public opinion research has been very much to downplay the significance of citizens' preferences on specific issues. Consider the arc of four separate areas of research in public opinion:

1. *Abundant Ignorance.* A popular segment of the former late-night institution *The Tonight Show with Jay Leno* featured the show's host approaching Los Angeles pedestrians at random and giving them an impromptu quiz. The laughs came when the hapless interviewees made wild misses concerning basic facts about politics, history, and pop culture. Who was Abraham Lincoln? The first president of the United States, of course. What two countries border the United

---

[7] As we finish this manuscript, gun control proponents have finally made a breakthrough. On June 25, 2022, a few weeks after a racist mass killing of ten people in Buffalo, NY followed by a separate killing of nineteen children and two adults at Robb Elementary School in Uvalde, TX, President Biden signed the Bipartisan Safer Communities Act. This law provides support for individuals experiencing mental health issues and strengthens "red flag laws." It does not enact many other restrictions favored by larger majorities of Americans – restrictions on assault weapons and limits on magazine capacity, for two examples.

States? Australia and Hawaii. What French emperor has a pastry named after him? Crème Brûlée. And so forth.

To be sure, the *Jaywalking* segments reflected soaring heights of citizen ignorance. But the central tendency is not very impressive either. One comprehensive review documented that Americans have passable knowledge of political institutions and processes (e.g. whether the Supreme Court has the power of judicial review). But their knowledge of specific people and events was mediocre at best (Delli-Carpini & Keeter 1997). The same goes for specifics about particular policies (Galston 2001; Gilens 2001), especially when the policies are affected by recent events (Barabas et al. 2014). These reliable results are an inauspicious beginning for issue public voting. If most Americans cannot say how long a Senate term is, or describe in broad strokes even the most prominent legislative proposals of the day, how could they possibly have meaningful opinions about specific, narrow policy areas?[8]

2. *Over-time Instability.* Not only are Americans short on facts, their views on particular issues change, sometimes drastically, over time. Converse documented in his famous (1964) essay that only 65 percent of survey respondents – only a bit more than chance – placed themselves on the same side of a given policy issue over a four-year span. The same basic result has been replicated several times since (Markus & Converse 1979; Kinder 1998, 793–797).[9] For instance, the 1984 iteration of the American National Election Study (ANES) asked Americans whether or not the government should guarantee people a job and a good standard of living. A few weeks later, it contacted the same people and asked the same question again. Forty-six percent of respondents gave a different answer the second time the question was asked (Page & Shapiro 1992, 6). How likely is it that citizens engage in issue-based voting if they cannot even keep track of what their issue opinions are?

3. *Framing Effects.* It gets worse still. Citizens' issue stances change sharply over just a few weeks, but they also change in response to small (sometimes trivial) changes in wording or emphasis – what researchers commonly call "framing effects" (Chong & Druckman 2007). Framing effects can often be demonstrated with simple question wording experiments. For instance, people are much more likely to support federal spending that is labeled "assistance to the poor" than "welfare" (Rasinski 1989). They are less tolerant of inflation when it is presented as raising employment than reducing unemployment

---

[8] Iyengar (1990) points to an important caveat. He examines issue-specific knowledge and finds knowledge in one area to be poorly predictive of knowledge in other areas, hinting at the possibility that general knowledge measures could miss substantial domain-specific knowledge. See Pérez (2015) for a similar point applied to ethnic politics.

[9] See Feldman (1989) for a thorough discussion of different ways to interpret these patterns.

(Druckman 2004). They are much more likely to say that the United States should "not allow" public speeches against democracy than that it should "forbid" public speeches against democracy. Results like these – and the examples abound – throw cold water on the notion of issue voting because they imply that many issue preferences that people report in surveys are illusory – the product of how a question was asked or what considerations happened to be salient, more than anything real in a person's head.

4. *Partisanship.* Finally, the prospects for issue-based voting face a substantial challenge from what political scientists have discovered about the nature of partisanship. Early survey researchers noted that learning whether a person thinks of themselves as a Republican or Democrat will often tell you a lot about how they feel about issues of the day (Campbell et al. 1960, ch. 6). It will also tell you – at least with high confidence – how they voted in recent presidential and congressional elections (Bartels 2000). These associations do not *inherently* challenge the notion that issue opinions influence political judgments. Perhaps people develop issue preferences first, and then decide which party they will identify with on that basis (Page & Brody 1972; Carsey & Layman 2006; Johnston 2006, for discussions). But partisanship appears to be a powerful political identity, often deeply connected to a person's self-concept (Greene 1990; Green et al. 2002; Huddy et al. 2015; Mason 2018). As such, it, more than issue positions, is likely to be the "unmoved mover" that represents the core determinant of political judgments.

Determining the causal precedence of partisanship vis-à-vis issue positions represents a tricky inferential problem (Fowler 2020, for a recent discussion), but several studies have accumulated compelling evidence that partisan considerations determine citizens' issue positions – at least under many circumstances. For instance, Cohen (2003) conducted a series of experiments in which participants read vignettes that described specific policies (e.g. a welfare reform that was either generous or stringent, as determined by a random assignment) and which party advocated for the policy (Republicans or Democrats) and found that party cues influenced participants' support much more than policy substance. Lenz (2012) examines a number of instances in which panel surveys repeated measures of party identification and issue positions at several points in time. He finds that exogenous events, such as an issue becoming a focal campaign topic, cause citizens to bring their issue preference into alignment with their party identification – rather than vice versa. Thus, we regard the evidence that people *commonly* determine their issue positions via partisan cues to be strong.[10]

---

[10] See also Druckman (2001), Kam (2005), and Brader et al. (2013). Bullock (2011) extends Cohen's experiments, and finds that policy information matters a lot more when there are more policy details available. But more recent work showing that partisan loyalty of trumps

Each of the four topics we review here represents a major area of public opinion research, and they lead to some of the field's hallmark findings. Jointly, they have led researchers to dour conclusions about the prospects of issue-based voting. For instance, one landmark review (Kinder 1998) calls citizens "unsophisticated in the extreme" (793) and argues that political judgments flow from affinity and animosity toward various groups, much more than anything resembling ideology or policy desires. More recently, Achen and Bartels' much-discussed book, *Democracy for Realists* (2016), argues that citizens are not suited to hold politicians accountable. It contains an entire section titled "The Illusion of 'Issue Voting'" (41), suggesting that voters tend to have issue preferences in sync with the politicians they support because the voter is taking a cue from a politician they like – not because they chose to support that politician on the basis of policy views. In conclusion, a major upshot of several decades of research in public opinion – quite distinct from the interest group literature above – is that issue preferences are mostly epiphenomenal. They are arbitrary statements made up on the fly, or byproducts of more fundamental group-based conflicts.

Unfulfilled Promise

The literatures reviewed above provide plenty of reason to doubt that "issues," understood as a category, influence the average citizen's political judgments very much. But the issue public hypothesis is narrower than that. It is that discrete issues each have their own constituencies for whom issue opinions influence *related* judgments. Considered one at a time, these constituencies might be quite small. But as the number of distinct political issues is large, so might the aggregate number of people who are – in one form or another – issue voters also be large. Can this more specific claim stand up to the mountain of evidence we allude to above? We think it plausibly can.

This possibility has cropped up here and there in survey research. Jon Krosnick and various collaborators have published several papers discussing how a social psychology literature on attitude intensity (Petty & Krosnick 1995) can help illuminate how policy preferences affect citizens' thoughts and behavior – an agenda explicitly linked to Converse's notion of issue publics (e.g. Krosnick 1990). Hutchings (2003) argues that issue publics (operationalized in a different way, as we discuss in Section 3) function as sleeping giants, in the sense that they can be activated by campaigns that focus on personally important issues.

---

commitment to democratic principles (e.g. Claassen & Ensley 2015; Graham & Svolik 2020; Simonovitz et al. 2022) leaves little doubt that people turn to partisan cues to resolve impulses that lead to conflicting judgments. See Lodge & Taber (2013) for a thorough treatment of the psychological bases of motivated reasoning in politics.

Hillygus and Shields (2008) show that campaigns can peel voters away from their partisan leanings by highlighting personally important issues on which the voter departs from the party line. These are all important contributions, and the implications for understanding the political system as a whole are potentially profound. Given this, it is surprising that issue publics are not a more focal area of research in public opinion than they are. For one sign of the modest extent to which the topic has taken hold, consider that a recent, nearly 400-page edited volume seeking to provide an overview of the state of public opinion research allocates only five paragraphs to the topic (Berinsky 2016).[11]

We suggest that a key reason that public opinion research has diverged from research about how groups influence public policy is the insufficient tools that public opinion researchers have used to identify and examine issue publics. In our next section, we turn to the difficult issue of measuring issue publics.

3 Issues of Measurement

We argue that one reason research on issue publics has proceeded inconsistently is that public opinion researchers have never had a fully satisfying approach for identifying membership in issue publics. Here, we present an abstract definition of an issue public to serve as standard against which to evaluate existing measurement approaches. We propose that an issue public is a group of citizens whose political judgments are influenced by a longstanding and emotionally charged psychological investment in a specific political topic. Then, we review four different approaches that have been employed in the past. For each, we highlight significant limitations, each of which would lead researchers to underappreciate the importance of issue publics.

What Is an Issue Public?

A starting point for evaluating a social scientific measure is to describe, in the abstract, what it is that we wish to measure. In our case, what *is* an issue public? A challenge in answering this question is that Converse's original treatment never defined the term precisely. The closest he comes is to remark (referring to Black Americans with a dated term) that:

---

[11] When the topic of issues publics does come up, several researchers have remarked on the potential significance of the idea. Martin Gilens closes the above-referenced five paragraphs by noting that the public's capacity to fulfill its "assigned role in democratic governance" hinges in no small part on the nature of issue publics (Gilens 2019, 47). Gabriele Lenz notes that issue publics might represent a major departure from his conclusions about whether citizens lead or follow, but laments the absence of a measurement approach adequate for assessing this possibility – what he calls "an embarrassment for the field of survey research" (Lenz 2012, 120).

different controversies excite different people to the point of real opinion formation. One man takes an interest in policies bearing on the Negro and is relatively
indifferent to or ignorant about controversies in other areas. His neighbor may
have few crystallized opinions on the race issue, but he may find the subject of
foreign aid very important. Such sharp divisions of interest are part of what the
term 'issue public' is intended to convey. (Converse 1964, 246)

There are several components here: an emotional component ("excite"),[12] a hint
that issue public members will attend to goings on related to their topic of
interest, and the idea that their opinions are "real" and "crystalized." In a nearby
passage, it becomes clear that over-time stability is another part of what
Converse is getting at.[13]

Reading how Converse used the term and how it has been invoked since, we
came up with three specific criteria to define an issue public. Most important, being
an issue public member is primarily an affective orientation based on caring about
an issue. More than that, it implies that a person cares about a particular issue
relative to others: if a person cares about issue X because they are attentive to
politics and care about basically all issues, we have not identified an issue public
member.

Second, the term "issue public" refers to people whose interest is *long-
standing* – things that a person pays attention to across contexts, and including
when the issue is not in the national spotlight. A person might care immensely
about health care on Monday as Congress considers reform legislation, and
about immigration on Tuesday, as the president tweets about it. This might be
genuine caring, but it would also be event-driven caring, and not the sort of
thing that the term "issue public" conveys.

Third, and stepping away from Converse, issue publics are groups of people
whose political judgments are significantly influenced by their issue public
attitudes. If we identify people who care about an issue, attend to it day in
and day out, but who are not influenced by it when they comment on public
affairs, decide for whom to vote, or engage in other politically significant acts,
we have not yet found an issue public.

At first blush, the last criterion might seem to introduce a tautology: we
cannot test the hypothesis that issue public attitudes influence judgments, since
influencing judgments is part of what it means to be an issue public. We prefer to
think of the criterion as a way to set a high standard for an issue public measure:

---

[12] A component that nicely parallels Markus Prior's (2019) conception of political interest.
Specifically, he writes about how "dispositional" interest in politics is maintained over time in
part because it is emotionally arousing.
[13] See footnote 43 in Converse (1964).

we are asking it to identify groups that are *politically significant* within the context of the broader political system – not mere attitudinal curiosities.[14]

Existing Approaches and Their Problems

Over the years, researchers have used a variety of methods to identify personally important issues. For the most part, however, they have relied on measures included on a survey with some other primary purpose in mind. We think this reality has restricted the scholarly understanding of issue publics in important and underappreciated ways. Our exposition in this section was influenced, we wish to stress, by an outstanding – but never published – dissertation on the topic (Gershkoff 2006). When we stumbled across and began to peruse Gershkoff's work, we realized that she beat us by several years in identifying and articulating several of our nascent concerns about survey research related to issue publics – plus some other ones that had not occurred to us. What follows is partly a summary and update of Gershkoff's critique.

1. *Interest Imputation*. One approach to identifying issue public members is to identify politically relevant groups, and assume that members of a particular group have certain consequent political interests. For instance, Hutchings (2003) supposes that union members represent an issue public for labor issues. More recently, Guntermann and Lenz (2022) consider whether individuals who contracted Covid-19, or who know someone who did, represent an issue public for pandemic issues.[15] The main appeal of the interest imputation approach is its feasibility. Researchers can often make a colorable argument that items included on a survey capture issue interests – even if the items were included for some different reason.

Unfortunately, the issue imputation approach is likely to generate a large number of false positives and false negatives. For instance, a person might deeply care about labor issues not because she is a union member herself, but because her friend or relative is a union member, or because she is sympathetic to workers. By the same token, a person can be a union member and *not* care very much about labor issues.[16] We fear that the noise inherent in this

---

[14] This approach aligns us to some extent with Hanretty et al. (2020). These authors identify personally important issues by examining their ability to influence votes for hypothetical candidates for the UK Parliament. They examine thirty-four issues and find that several issues that are not currently focal in political discourse have the potential to influence votes.

[15] See also Bolsen and Leeper (2013) for a study that uses interest imputation to predict attention to group-relevant news stories. Henderson (2013) finds that seniors paid more attention to Social Security news in the 2000 Presidential Campaign than non-seniors.

[16] As a graduate student, one of the authors of this element was required to join and pay dues to a union as a condition of becoming a course instructor. But he has no particular interest in labor policy. Similarly, one of the authors' fathers worked at a grocery store in his twenties where all of

measurement approach might be quite substantial. For instance, how closely, really, does interest in the abortion issue track with being a woman between the ages of eighteen and forty? (See Price & Zaller 1993, 154) To this point, Claassen and Nicholson (2013) compare the issue opinions of people with a *potential* stake in specific outcomes (e.g. being over fifty for the issue of privatizing Social Security) to people who explicitly joined a political organization (e.g. the AARP). They find substantial differences, with views among joiners being more extreme.

The issue imputation approach also narrows which issues can be examined, since many issues do not clearly map onto individuals' objective characteristics. What class of individuals could one assume represents the issue public for foreign interventions, net neutrality issues, animal welfare, vaccine mandates, gun violence, free speech protections, or any number of other important topics?

2. *Most Important Problem*. A second approach that has been used to assess issue interest is to ask survey respondents, in open-ended format, "What do you think is the most important problem facing the country today?" Survey firms like Gallup ask this question regularly, and it has also been used to identify issue public membership (e.g. Maggioto & Piereson 1978; Aldrich et al. 1989). A significant drawback of this approach is that it might mistake *accessibility* – a topic being prominent in a person's mind, perhaps because it is receiving news coverage – for long-run *caring* about an issue. This mismatch is particularly likely given that the question asks about a problem "facing the country today." (Contrast this phrasing with "facing you, day in and day out.") A second concern is that recognizing that something is a "problem" is not the same thing as caring about it. In a thorough analysis, Wlezien examines these issues and concludes that the most important problem question is a "fundamentally flawed" measure of issue importance (2005, 556; see also Johns 2010).

3. *Counting Open-Ended Responses*. Following her critique of the methods discussed in Sections 3.1 and 3.2, Gershkoff (2006) offers an alternative – what she calls the Counting Open-Ended Responses (COR) technique. The COR technique relies on three open-ended questions: one about things a person likes and dislikes about major party presidential candidates; one about things a person

---

the workers were required to be dues-paying members of a union. The union launched multiple strikes that he felt were frivolous and extracted concessions that were so paltry that many workers lost significantly more in wages from the strike than they stood to gain later. This, among other experiences in the union, fostered anti-union attitudes that he still holds over thirty years later. In both examples, researchers relying on imputation would have generated false positives.

likes and dislikes about the two major political parties; and one asking a person to list up to three most important problems facing the country. These three questions have appeared on several iterations of the ANES. Gershkoff (2006) counts up how many times across all of these questions a particular political issue is mentioned. To the extent a single topic is mentioned multiple times, she takes it as a sign that that topic is a critical issue for a personal respondent.

We think this approach offers a lot that other approaches do not. As shall become clear when we elaborate on our own approach in Section 4, we think that unprompted mentions of a single topic are indeed a strong sign that an issue is important to a person. However, we are concerned that the particular referents – likes and dislikes about presidential candidates and political parties – serve to constrain the range of topics that respondents will mention. In particular, respondents will likely mention topics that have been focal in the presidential campaign, since these topics are a more reasonable basis to like or dislike the candidates and parties. They will be unlikely to mention topics such as marijuana policy or animal rights – issues that might be personally important, but which simply are not focal in the presidential campaign.

Simply put, we think the COR method is based on sound principles, but it somewhat restricted by its reliance on measures that happened to land on the ANES questionnaire. It is not the approach one would likely employ if given the liberty to design a measure from the ground up.

4. *Issue-specific Importance Questions.* The final approach we review draws from a social psychology literature on attitude intensity (Petty & Krosnick 1995). The starting point for this approach is the sort of questions about specific political issues that are common fare on public opinion surveys – questions like: "Do you favor, oppose, or neither favor nor oppose an amendment to the U.S. Constitution banning marriage between two people who are the same sex?"[17] On academic surveys, a question like this will commonly have five or seven response options capturing gradations of attitude intensity. For instance, respondents who answered this question when it was presented on the ANES could indicate that they favored such an amendment "a little," "moderately," or "a great deal" (with symmetrical response options on the "oppose" side of the issue) – or they could indicate full neutrality ("neither favor nor oppose"). Answers to such questions are commonly called an individual's attitude *extremity* – though the term attitude *position* is sometimes used synonymously (e.g. Taber et al. 2009).

---

[17] The question comes from the 2008–2009 ANES Panel Study, available at https://electionstudies .org/data-center/2008-2009-panel-study/.

Attitude extremity often carries a sort of privileged status, since it character-izes the substance of an individual's attitude on a particular topic. It is often conceptualized spatially, with proponents and opponents to a particular issue existing at opposite ends of a continuum. The crux of the attitude literature, though, is that attitude extremity can be distinguished from an array of other attributes – the extent to which an attitude is crystallized, elaborated, certain, or morally convicted, to name a few (Visser et al. 2006, for a review). Key for our purposes, one secondary dimension of attitude intensity – personal importance – has commonly been invoked to identify issue publics in public opinion surveys (e.g. Krosnick 1990). In this approach, after an attitude extremity question, a respondent would furthermore be asked, "How important is this issue to you personally?" with response options (often four or five) ranging from "not at all important" to "extremely important."

The major advantage of this approach, compared to interest imputation, is that it comes closer to the construct of interest: caring about a political topic is a key part of issue public membership. Unlike interest imputation, it can be applied to any topic, and it allows interest to crop up in places that would otherwise be missed, such as a man who cares about abortion policy, or a white person who cares about racial equality. However, this approach also has some drawbacks. For one thing, social desirability pressures might lead people to overstate their level of interest. For instance, a person might indicate substantial caring about tax policy – even though she never thinks about it – simply because this seems like something a good citizen should do (Hanretty et al. 2020).

A second, but related, drawback is that the personal importance question might fail to distinguish substantial from immense levels of interest. The personal importance question typically has five response options: the issue is "extremely," "very," "moderately," "slightly," or "not at all" personally import-ant. A word like "extremely" is open to interpretation, and we suspect that respondents often interpret it in a broader way than would be ideal for deter-mining who is a member of an issue public. To be sure, a person who follows a particular policy area assiduously (think of Eldon Gould – from Section 1 – on trade policy) will likely say that that topic is extremely important to him. But another person might indicate that a topic is extremely personally important simply because the topic seems important in the abstract, or because it seems like something that could one day have material implications for her life.

A Critique of Closed-ended Personal Importance Items

Asking issue-specific importance questions is the most well-established approach for identifying issue publics. As such, we allocate some extra space to consider its drawbacks. To do so, we draw on the 2008–2009 American National Election Panel Study. Although slightly dated, this resource has features that are extremely helpful for our purposes. First, it is a large, compensated, nationally representative sample conducted in the midst of a presidential election.[18] Second – and quite rare – it presented closed-ended issue importance questions – for several issues – to the same respondents, at two different points in time.

In January, respondents were asked their opinions about nine issues that were likely to be focal in the presidential campaign: a constitutional amendment banning same-sex marriage; the US government paying the cost of prescription drugs for senior citizens living on very little income; the US government paying for all necessary medical care for all Americans; the US government holding terrorist suspects in prison without criminal charges (a question about the right of habeas corpus); the US government needing a court order before listening in on Americans' phone calls; allowing illegal immigrants to work in the United States for three years (a question about work visas); allowing illegal immigrants a path to citizenship; raising federal income taxes on people who make more than $200,000 per year; and raising federal income taxes on people who make less than $200,000 per year. Then, seven months later (in October), eight of these questions were presented again. (The omitted topic was about taxes for people making under $200,000 per year.) This design allows for a comparison of how issue importance perceptions change, within individuals, over an extended period of time. For each topic, respondents were also asked how important the issue was to them personally, on a scale with five response options: not at all important; slightly important; moderately important; very important; and extremely important.[19]

Figure 1 shows the distribution of responses to these questions, in the January 2008 wave. The figure illustrates that Americans' responses tend toward the high end of the response scale. In fact, for seven of the nine issues (same sex marriage and taxes for those making over $200,000 being the exceptions), the median response is "very important." Figure 2 makes a related point. It shows the distribution of how many issues respondents deemed to be at least "very" important to them personally. The median (and modal) response is to stipulate six of the nine

---

[18] Details on the 2008–2009 ANES Panel Study are available at https://electionstudies.org/data-center/2008-2009-panel-study/.

[19] There were 1,623 respondents in the January wave, 1,381 of whom also completed the October wave. However, the policy battery analyzed here was only presented to 50 percent of respondents (chosen at random) in the October wave. As such, the analytical sample size for analyses focused on January only are approximately 1,600, while those focused on January/October change are approximately 700. (Counts for specific analyses vary slightly due to item nonresponse.)

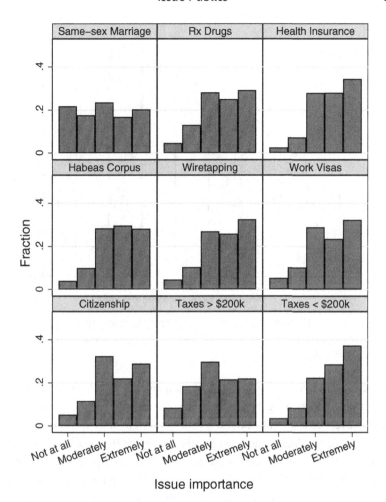

Figure 1 Personal importance ascribed to nine issues on the ANES
Note: Panels are histograms showing the distribution of responses to personal import-
ance questions, for nine topics examined in the January 2008 wave of the American
National Election Panel Study.

issues to be at least "very" personally important. Only 4.9 percent of respondents
indicate that zero issues are personally important.

One might take these patterns at face value – inferring that many Americans
really do personally care about many of the issues that the ANES survey presented.
This interpretation seems unlikely, however, given that several of the issues directly
affect only small slices of the population. The interpretation is also hard to square
with the prevailing wisdom – discussed in Section 2 – that most Americans are low
in political knowledge and pay cursory attention to public affairs. In fact, we can
see the inconsistency play out within this very study. Consider the respondents who

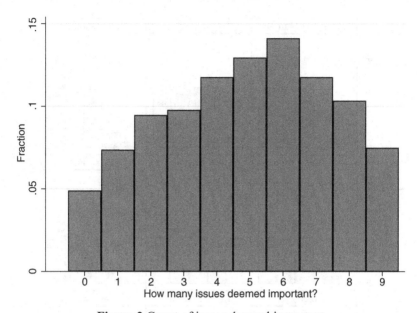

Figure 2 Count of issues deemed important

This figure is a histogram of the count of issues (out of nine) deemed at least "very" important, for each respondent.

indicated at least five issues to be personally important. Even within this group – to outward appearances, a highly engaged bunch – the level of political knowledge is unimpressive. For instance, based on questions asked in other waves of the study, 60.0 percent did not know that the length of a term in the House of Representatives was two years, 61.9 percent did not know that the term for a United States Senator was six years, and 33.0 percent could not identify John McCain's former occupation (serving in the US military) from a list of four possibilities.

More likely, then, distributions such as those seen in Figure 1 drastically overstate the proportion of Americans who personally care about specific issues. We suspect such measures are afflicted by acquiescence bias – the tendency to agree with propositions presented in a survey – as well as social desirability pressures – a respondent's desire to present themselves as an attentive and engaged citizen.[20]

---

[20] Rabinowitz et al. (1982) offer a clever remedy for this problem. They ask respondents to rate fifteen issues on a scale ranging from "not important to you" to "very important to you." Then, they ask respondents which issue was the most important, from among those rated "very" important. This approach addresses acquiescence bias to some extent, since it identifies a single issue of particular importance. It also ensures that the most important issue is one that the respondent does care about, since the follow-up question is limited to those rated as very important. However, it still constrains the range of issues that get asked about – a problem that will be our focus in Section 4. Rabinowitz et al. (1982) find that personally important issues, measured this way, do influence presidential candidate evaluations more than other issues.

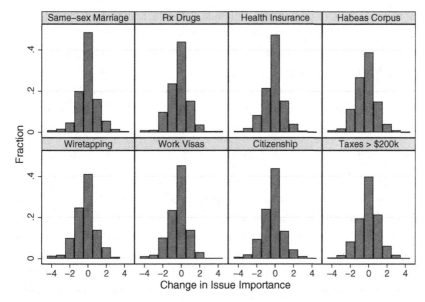

Figure 3 Change in issue-specific personal importance, January to October
Change in issue-specific personal importance measures, October 2008 ratings minus
January 2008 ratings. The taxes on nonwealthy individual questions were not asked in
October, so are omitted.

One important criterion for an issue public measure is over-time reliability. Issue
publics are, by our definition, *durable* groupings. This is an important part of what
would make them politically consequential. Thus, if the closed-ended issue importance measures capture what they aspire to capture, over-time change should be
modest. Figure 3 examines over-time reliability by presenting the distributions of
issue-specific changes in personal importance over time – the October 2008 wave
minus the January 2008 wave. Here, positive values indicate issues that became
more important over time, and negative values indicate issues that became less
important.

The key result in Figure 3 is that issue importance ratings are fairly unstable over
time. In fact, for none of the eight issues do even 50 percent of respondents provide
the same answer that they did ten months earlier. One could plausibly chalk such
a result up to the increasing intensity of the presidential campaign – except that
decreases in personal importance outnumber increases (34.8 percent compared to
21.5 percent, pooling across issues). Pooling across all issues, the Pearson correlation between January personal importance and October issue importance is
a moderate 0.55.

Another criterion by which to evaluate the closed-ended importance items
is their ability to predict stability in a person's underlying issue attitude.

For instance, when a person says, in January, that their opinion about same-sex marriage is personally important, are they more likely to have the same opinion about same-sex marriage when reinterviewed in October? (More likely, that is, than someone who, in January, said that their opinion about same-sex marriage was not personally important.) We examine this attribute of the closed-ended importance items as well, by estimating the following regression model:

$$|\text{IssuePosition}_{Oct} - \text{IssuePosition}_{Jan}| = \beta_0 + \beta_1 \text{IssueImportance}_{Jan} + \beta_{2-7} \text{PositionDummies} + \varepsilon. \quad (1)$$

In plain English, we estimate the magnitude of a respondent's issue position change (January compared to October) as a function of the importance they ascribe to that issue. We also include a dummy variable for each of the issue stances a respondent could have taken in January. These dummies serve two purposes. First, they contend with problems that routinely arise when using bounded attitude scales to examine over-time change: extreme opinions have a greater theoretical potential to change (six units, compared to just three for a neutral opinion) and will be more likely to change, due to regression to the mean. The second purpose is to set a fair standard for the importance measures: they merit inclusion on a survey instrument only if they provide information *above and beyond* that which would already be captured by asking a respondent their issue position. Otherwise, researcher could simply rely on the extremity of a respondent's issue attitude as a proxy for how important it is. By including these dummies in our regression model, we are examining the importance measures' value-added.

Figure 4 summarizes the results by reporting the predicted magnitude of change for low and high values of issue importance. As the figure shows, six of the relationships run in the expected direction: people for whom the issue is personally important exhibit less attitude change than those for whom it is not important. However, the Same-sex Marriage and Work Visas issues run in the opposite direction. Of the six correctly signed relationships, only one (the Taxes issue) is statistically significant at the $p < 0.05$ level. Thus, the closed-ended measures appear to predict over-time attitude stability weakly at best.

These shortcomings might be overlooked if closed-ended issue importance measures helped to prognosticate political behavior. It is conceivable that they would. Acquiescence bias and social desirability pressures might inflate the mean of each item, but variation relative to that mean (such as a respondent choosing to mark an issue as "extremely" rather than "very" personally important) might still be informative. Erratic change over time could represent random measurement error, in which case statistical models might help filter signal from noise. For these reasons, as a final examination of the closed-ended issue

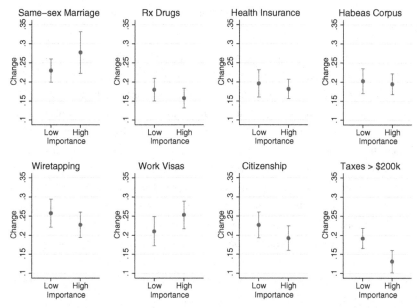

Figure 4 Personal importance weakly predicts attitude stability
Points represent the predicted magnitude of attitude change (from October to January)
for each of eight issues, based on model (1). For predicted values, issue importance is set
to its minimum and maximum levels. Whiskers represent 95 percent confidence intervals, derived from robust standard errors.

importance measures, we examine their ability to predict the quintessential
political action: choosing for whom to vote.

Because George W. Bush was term limited, the 2008 presidential election
had open primaries for both the Republican and Democratic nominations. By
Super Tuesday, the Republican contest had narrowed to two major contend-
ers: John McCain and Mitt Romney. (Romney withdrew after a disappointing
showing on Super Tuesday.) The Democratic contest was one for the ages.
For months, Hillary Clinton narrowly trailed Barack Obama's delegate count
and hoped that uncommitted superdelegates could deliver the nomination to
her. She stayed in the race until the final primary elections were held, and
Obama clinched the delegate count needed to become the nominee, on
June 3. And of course, Obama defeated McCain in the general election on
November 4.

We examine the extent to which personally important issue opinions predicted voting in each of these three contests: between Romney and McCain
among Republican primary voters; between Obama and Clinton among
Democratic primary voters; and between McCain and Obama among general
election voters. To do so, we estimate the following logistic regression model:

Vote choice $= \beta_0 + \beta_1 \text{Opinion} + \beta_2 \text{Importance} + \beta_3 \text{Opinion} \times \text{Importance} + \beta_{4-n} \text{Controls} + \varepsilon.$ (2)

In this model, vote choice is a binary variable that $= 1$ if the respondent voted for McCain (for the Republican Primary or General Election models) or $= 1$ if the respondent voted for Obama (in the Democratic primary model). We estimate relationships for a respondent's issue opinion (always coded so a conservative opinion takes high values), the personal importance they ascribe to that opinion, and the interaction of these two variables. Our primary interest is in this interaction, as it reflects the extent to which the effect of an issue opinion *depends* on whether the respondent cares about that issue or not. Following convention, we include controls for party identification, gender, education, race, income, and age.

In some cases, it is straightforward to predict how a particular issue might affect vote choices. For instance, Obama was generally regarded as having more progressive credibility than Clinton: he opposed the Iraq war, which Clinton voted to authorize as a senator, and he made sweeping reform of the country's health-care system a centerpiece of his campaign. In other cases, it is more difficult: the ideological difference between McCain and Romney were subtle and idiosyncratic, though McCain had more of a track record of working for immigration reform. Issue-specific predictions are, however, secondary to our objective: determining whether the issue importance questions included on the ANES Panel study help distinguish which issue opinions bear on vote choice more than others. We opt to examine *all* the relationships available to us, to see if the personal importance measures *ever* distinguish more influential opinions from less influential ones. We estimate our model for each of nine issues, and for each of the three contests, for twenty-seven models in total.

We report all regressions in the appendix, Tables C1 through C3. The key results, however, are straightforward to summarize. Across these twenty-seven models, there are only two statistically significant (two-tailed $p < 0.05$) Opinion $\times$ Importance interactions. The first of these implies that opposing tax increases on Americans who make less than \$200,000 oriented individuals to vote for McCain rather than Romney in the Republican primary – if they deem this issue personally important. The second implies that favoring the suspension of habeas corpus– oriented individuals to vote for Clinton rather than Obama in the Democratic primary – again, if they deem this issue personally important. The personal importance measures do not appear to isolate significant differences in any of the general election models.

This is an uninspiring performance. Although we have ample statistical power – nearly 1,200 respondents in the general election models – and although we have examined nine issues in three different contexts, the personal importance measures hardly ever prognosticate for whom issues will weigh more heavily on vote choice. It bears notice, also, that we have examined both a context wherein partisan pressures are neutralized (a primary election) and one where partisan pressures are strong, but the candidates exhibit starker divides on the issues (the general election). This is not to say that the personal importance measures are *never* a valuable inclusion on a survey instrument.[21] But in this circumstance – one that seems ideal for them to prove their mettle – they appear to fall short.[22]

What we are left with, then, is a potentially indispensable concept – issues publics – and no satisfying way to measure it. In our next section, we propose and test a new approach.

4 A New Approach

One thing all four approaches described in Section 3 have in common is that they attempt to assess issue public membership with existing survey measures that were designed for some other purpose. As a starting point for our investigation, we asked ourselves: What would an issue public measure look like, if designed from the ground up?

We decided that we did not want to predefine a set of issues that respondents might particularly care about. We worried that doing so would go too far in imposing our own sense of what issues are likely to be regarded as important – issues with substantial national coverage, for instance – and we did not want to limit the measurement space in this way. Instead, we wanted a more inductive approach that would allow respondents to say for themselves what issues are important. For this reason, we decided to develop an open-ended measure.

We also sought to develop a measure that takes the abstract concept of an issue public as its starting point. Recall from Section 3 the three criteria we argued are critical to the concept of an issue public: members of an issue public should care about that issue more than most others; their interest should be durable over time; and their issue attitudes should be politically influential. Based on these considerations, we wrote the following question:

> Some people have a political issue that they care about more than most other issues. They might think about the issue a lot. They might pay particular attention

---

[21] Indeed, one of us has found elsewhere that the personal importance items are helpful for predicting activism and engagement on specific issues, as well as to compare and contrast with other facets of attitude strength (Ryan 2014; 2017; 2019; Delton, DeScioli & Ryan 2020).

[22] A dissertation by Madson (2021) provides some additional data points. Madson uses personal importance measures included on other iterations of the ANES and examines whether these moderate the priming and learning effects described by Lenz (2012). Madson concludes that "there is minimal to no moderating effect" (40).

> to news about that issue, even when it's not making national news. They might
> focus on what political candidates say about that issue, and decide who to vote
> for on the basis of that issue. Or they might just care about the issue a lot.
>   Is there an issue like that for you?

Respondents simply answered "Yes" or "No." Those who answered "Yes"
would be presented a straightforward open-ended question as a follow up:

> In just a sentence or two, what issue is it that you care about?

This combination of questions, we posited, has the potential to reveal a face of
issue-based voting that is not usually captured on public opinion surveys.

One possible concern about our approach is that we are playing fast and loose
with best practices in the formulation of survey questions. The first question we
presented is multifaceted (or "double barreled"). It alludes to frequency of thought,
attention to news, attention to candidate statements, and influence on judgment, all
in the same paragraph. While true, "caring" is clearly elevated above the other
factors via the first and last sentences. Moreover, we thought the additional
illustrations would help respondents understand the particular kind of mental
significance that we hope to capture. In doing so, we aim to reduce the likelihood
of false positives whereby respondents say they care about something merely to
demonstrate they are an attentive citizen (social desirability) or to say they care
about an issue because *other* people care about it at the moment.

Putting the Measure to the Test

To determine whether the approach described in the previous section sheds new
light on issue publics, we included it in two public opinion surveys. First, we
designed and fielded, via Amazon.com's Mechanical Turk crowdsourcing service, a three-wave study that unfolded from August 2018 to January 2019.
Second, we included our instrumentation on two waves of the Politics in the
Field at UNC (PFUNC) study – a multi-investigator study designed by
researchers at the University of North Carolina at Chapel Hill – that were
fielded by Qualtrics in March and July of 2021.[23] Each data source has some
advantages relative to the other. The MTurk sample is a small convenience
sample and we make no claim that it reflects national demographics. However,
MTurk survey respondents are generally highly attentive (Hauser & Schwarz
2016), and we examine them at three separate points in time. The PFUNC study
is much larger and features a diverse national sample targeted to meet Census

---

[23] We had aspirations to conduct a national study more promptly following our MTurk study, but
the Covid-19 pandemic interfered with our timeline. The PFUNC study included prior survey
waves that were entirely unrelated to the research reported here. For simplicity, we refer to the
two waves that included our measures as Wave 1 and Wave 2.

benchmarks for gender, age, race, and education. However, space constraints required us to ask fewer questions. Additionally, and consistent with other comparisons across convenience samples and commercial platforms, we see somewhat lower respondent attentiveness in the PFUNC study (see Zhang & Gearhart 2020).[24] The MTurk study had 267 valid responses in Wave 1,[25] and the PFUNC study had 2,408 in Wave 1.

Recruitment and incentives. The MTurk study employed an incentive structure that we hoped would minimize attrition over the course of our study. The study's consent screen informed respondents that they would be paid $0.25 for their initial Wave 1 response – a low rate of compensation. However, they would be paid an additional $2.50 (as a bonus) if, in approximately three weeks, they completed Wave 2 of the study – fairly generous compensation for the total time commitment. Respondents had to confirm that they were interested in participating in a follow-up study, following this compensation scheme, in order to begin Wave 1. Of the 267 individuals invited to Wave 2, 202 completed it (plus six partial completions), for a response rate of 75.7 percent.

MTurk Wave 3 was not planned at the outset of our investigation. However, we were so encouraged by the low attrition going from Wave 1 to Wave 2, as well as our initial results, that we decided to contact the 267 subjects invited to Wave 2 again in January of 2019 – five months after our initial survey – and offer them an additional $2.50 bonus for completing an additional instrument. Even after this long delay, 172 respondents completed the instrument (plus 4 partial), for a response rate of 64.2 percent.

The PFUNC study is a rolling panel study. In this approach, the first individuals targeted for recruitment to a particular survey wave are those who completed the prior wave. However, the attrition rate among Qualtrics respondents is fairly high – often more than 50 percent, even when two survey waves are spaced less than one month apart. For this reason, after the individuals who

---

[24] This remark is based on the overall level of care respondents seem to put into the open-ended responses we describe below: it is noticeably lower for the PFUNC study than the MTurk study. The PFUNC study included one attention check question (on wave 2). The passage rate was fairly low: 55.5 percent.

[25] This study hit the field just as it was coming to light that bad actors in foreign countries were using Virtual Private Servers (VPSs) to mimic United States IP addresses and complete surveys available through MTurk (see Kennedy et al. 2020; Ahler et al. 2019). Indeed we found evidence of fraudulent responding in our study – concerning, since such responses are clearly not providing useful data (most appear not to understand English) and, moreover, outside the population of interest. However, we were able to identify and remove the vast majority of these responses. See Appendix C for the procedure. We expect that any fraudulent responses that we failed to identify would make it *more* difficult to identify issue publics, since the patterns we look for require careful and attentive responding. We have no reason to believe this issue affects our PFUNC data.

Table 1 Samples sizes and fielding dates

	Fielding dates	Complete responses
MTurk Study		
Wave 1	Aug. 1, 2018–Aug. 15, 2018	267
Wave 2	Sep. 7, 2018–Sep. 12, 2018	208
Wave 3	Jan. 18, 2019–Jan. 24, 2019	172
PFUNC		
Wave 1	March 18, 2021–April 6, 2021	2,408
Wave 2	July 28, 2021–August 26, 2021	2,466 (797 from Wave 1)

responded to the previous wave have been contacted several times, Qualtrics recruits new respondents until the target sample size for the current wave has been reached. Qualtrics uses targeted recruitment to construct a sample that matches Census benchmarks for major demographic characteristics. This approach has a weaker claim to being genuinely "nationally representative" than an approach grounded in random sampling, such as the ANES. However, it still leads to a sample that is diverse with respect to age, education, race, income, and sex (see Appendix A, Table A1).

Table 1 shows the fielding dates and sample sizes for our two studies. All MTurk respondents who completed Wave 2 or Wave 3 also completed Wave 1. For PFUNC, slightly more than 2,400 respondents completed each of the two waves, though only 797 of the Wave 2 respondents are repeats from Wave 1. Although this is a much higher attrition rate (67 percent), PFUNC still augments the data available considerably.

We organize the remainder of this section as a series of substantive questions about issue publics – each paired with a discussion of how our study provides new evidence relevant to answering them.

What Proportion of People Say They Belong to an Issue Public?

We begin at the simplest level: What proportion of respondents indicated that they had a personally important issue in response to our root issue public question? As Table 2 shows, in the MTurk dataset, 78.3 percent of respondents answered this question in the affirmative. In the PFUNC dataset, a lower percentage answered in the affirmative: 54.1 percent. Of course, some respondents answering in the affirmative might not actually be able to identify a specific political issue. Thus, a coder read all the open-ended responses that participants provided for our second, open-ended question (asking the respondent to write

Table 2 Percentage of respondents claiming IP membership

	MTurk (%)	*PFUNC* (%)
Answer in the affirmative	78.3	54.1
Identifiable issue	74.9	35.5
N	267	2,407

a sentence or two describing the issue they care about). We flagged responses that did not in fact name a specific political issue. As Table 2 shows, nearly all MTurk respondents (all but nine) who said they had a personally important issue were able to articulate one. There was considerably more falloff in the PFUNC survey. This pattern is consistent with our sense that MTurk respondents are more diligent and attentive than respondents recruited via major survey vendors (Zhang & Gearhart 2020).

Responses coded as not clearly articulating a specific political issue came in several different varieties, and it is worth a moment to describe some of them. First, some such responses interpreted the question in broader terms than we hoped. They offered general remarks about politics. Examples include:

"corruption in our government and the fact politians [sic.] refude [sic.] to listen to the people"
"My family and my friends that they are safe." [Perhaps a reference to the Covid-19 pandemic, but we are not sure.]
"Fairness to all people"

Second, there were numerous responses wherein a respondent *might* have a genuine issue public issue, but where – owing to a time-pressured or somewhat inarticulate respondent – we could not be confident enough to code them as such. Examples include:

"Law reform."
"I care about financial markets"
"LIBERTY! And how its [sic.] being extinguished like a match."
"There's many issues to worry about but what concerns me is how the country is being ran [sic.] and how this generation is going to waste."
"Catching it" [Again, possibly a reference to the Covid-19 pandemic.]
"Keeping the individuality of American citizens"
"Lots of different issues"

Third, some responses griped about current political actors, but did not mention any specific issues:

"How President Binden [sic.] is doing his job"
"Biden and his socialist globalist administration and left wingers
   destroying our country"
"trump constantly lying to the American citizens"

And fourth, some responses were totally inscrutable, or instances where the respondent used the free response box to grumble to the researchers:

"the issues are very calm to face and deal perfect"
"lengthy"
"Not enough enough [sic.] information"

We review these difficult cases to show that, in classifying whether a respondent articulated a specific issue or not, we have set a fairly high bar. Several responses we code as not identifying a specific issue *might* indeed be members of some issue public – but were not able or not inclined to demonstrate as much on our survey. Higher percentages of respondents might be *able* to describe an important issue – but they did not do so for us. In this sense, the percentages reported in the second row of Table 2 are conservative.

What Kinds of Issues Get Mentioned?

We wanted to get a sense of what topics come to respondents' minds when they are asked – with very little context – what political issue they care about. In particular, we wanted to examine how much *citizens'* perspectives on what kinds of issues are important coincides with *researchers'* perspectives. Political scientists and other researchers are likely to be highly attentive to current events. When they consider what political issues citizens might regard as important, their perspective is likely to be influenced by this focus. For instance, they might begin with a slate of issues that receive substantial attention in the news or in policy discussions, and examine how many citizens care about these topics. Or, they might unwittingly impose their own views on the quandary ("People *should* care about climate change."). The risks here are obvious: average citizens might develop their political interests in very different ways. They might have real and meaningful political interests – but ones that do not line up with topics that researchers expect to be personally important. In short, researchers might look for issue publics in the wrong place.

To gain some insight into how well-aligned citizens' and researchers' view of important issues are, we specified, before our MTurk survey, an ex ante list of fifteen issues (visible on the left side of Table 3) that we thought respondents might stipulate to be personally important. As Table 3 shows, the list includes both distributive and social issues. It includes several issues that are reliably focal in American political discourse (e.g. immigration, health care, abortion) as

Table 3 Proportion of respondents mentioning policy areas

MTurk		PFUNC	
Policy	Percent mentioning (%)	Policy	Percent mentioning (%)
Immigration	18.0	Immigration	11.8
Health care	13.0	Health care	11.1
Abortion	11.0	Abortion	6.3
Education	0.5	Education	1.3
The environment	13.0	The environment	9.5
Taxes	2.5	Taxes	2.5
Gun control	10.0	Gun control	3.9
Marijuana	4.5	Marijuana	0.5
Minimum wage	0.5	Minimum wage	0.2
Stem cell research	0.0	Electoral reform	4.9
Affordable housing	0.0	Media	1.2
Labor policy	0.0	Foreign policy	0.1
Offshore drilling	0.5	Covid−19	10.6
Public support for the arts	0.0	Race relations	7.9
Gen. Modified Organisms (GMOs)	0.0	Right-wing nationalism	0.8
Some other specific policy	**26.5**	**Some other specific policy**	**27.6**
Total	100.0		100.0
N	200		855

Note: Analysis is limited to respondents who provided an interpretable issue they cared about.

well as others that tend to bubble up and recede from time to time (e.g. minimum wage and marijuana regulation). In any event, our intention was to come up with a list that would capture as many of our participants' unprompted responses as we could, while still specifying reasonably *specific* issues (e.g. we excluded "the economy" as an item, since it arguably encompasses many more specific issues: tax policy, monetary policy, regulations, stimulus, minimum wage, and more.)

We revised this list before the PFUNC study. We dropped five issues that few people specified to be important, and we added six issues that seemed likely to come up, given current events. We added a category for race relations (the survey was fielded after nearly a year of intense protesting following the murder of George Floyd and several other racially charged episodes). We added three items prompted by the January 6, 2021, insurrection at the US Capitol and the events leading up to it: Right-wing nationalism, Electoral reform (anticipating complaints from conservative respondents about perceived electoral fraud), and the media (given Donald Trump's relentless griping about major news outlets covered his administration). We added a foreign policy category, given that issues related to Iran, China, and Afghanistan were all focal at this time. And we added a listing for the Covid-19 pandemic – for obvious reasons: the pandemic had interrupted American life for more than a year at this point, and vaccines were just starting to become widely available.

Some might consider these lists of issues and fairly question whether all the inclusions meet our own definition of an issue public. Particularly in the PFUNC list, some of the issues (e.g. the Covid-19 pandemic) are clearly event-driven.[26] However, we do not contend that all of the issues in Table 3 definitely represent issue publics. Some meet the characteristics better than others. Rather, our intention was to estimate an *upper bound* for how many open-ended responses we could predict ex ante. For this reason, we can be fairly confident that responses we failed to predict would be missed by the more structured measurement approaches we review in Section 3.

Table 3 reports what proportion of open-ended responses coincided with each topic we specified in advance.[27] Unsurprisingly, several major issues that have been focal in the news were mentioned by significant proportions of respondents. The key result in Table 3, however, is that, in both studies, upward of 26 percent of the named issues were ones that we did not predict. It is worth a moment to convey the breadth of concerns revealed in such issues. We do this in Table 4 by reporting twenty verbatim responses to the open-ended important issue question in the PFUNC dataset. While these examples were chosen for illustration – not at random – we feel they help to elucidate the frequently particularistic nature of citizens' policy concerns. We see mentions of

---

[26] A definitional question we avoid here is whether a group of citizens that is animated by an issue should still be regarded as an issue public if the issue itself is limited in term. (Covid-19 is an example. It has stayed on the political agenda for longer than we would have guessed, but still seems likely to fade as a major focus for public concern within a few years' time.) We suspect such term-limited issues can result in genuine issue voting. But they might not lead to the long-term systemic effects that have long been the focus of issue public theorizing.

[27] In this coding exercise, for a respondent's issue to be coded under a particular heading, we required the response to be at a similar level of generality as the pre-specified topic. For instance, a respondent who said that they care about "I care about the state of healthcare in this country" would be classified under the "Health Care" heading. But a respondent who said they care about "The mental illness crisis and the addictions it causes" would not, since this is a far more specific topic than is conveyed by the term "Health Care." We elaborate on this issue of generality as an important measurement consideration below.

Alzheimer's, gender disparities in the judicial system, homelessness, dog health, and several other colorful topics.[28] In short, these results hint that there exists a substantial proportion of citizens who might have influential political concerns that researchers could easily miss.

Inspecting open-ended responses revealed another way in which citizens' and researchers' view of political issues could be misaligned. For reasons of analytical simplicity, researchers might be impelled to distill possible areas of issue focus into a manageable number of broad headings, as we have done in Table 3. But as Table 4 shows, in several cases, the open-ended responses suggested that citizens' points of interest were more specific than these headings reflect. The respondent who cared about "Type one diabetes" is a good example. Arguably, this response belongs to the Health Care heading. But it is a far more specific response than that heading implies. The person who wrote the response might be attentive to specific facets of a political candidate's health-care platform in a way that merely thinking of them as attending to health care would leave out. We return to this matter later.[29]

What Sorts of People Join Issue Publics?

In a democracy, political influence depends on who shows up to participate. Thus, a thematic concern in much political behavior research is that political influence would become stratified by citizens' material resources (e.g. Verba et al. 1995), gender (e.g. Burns et al. 2001), knowledge (e.g. Althaus 1998), or intrinsic political interest (e.g. Prior 2019). A particularly palpable concern, given the high current level of political polarization, is that political engagement is stratified by the posture one takes toward political disagreement – with more engaged citizens also being more likely to harbor adversarial and contemptuous views toward political opponents (Krupnikov & Ryan 2022).

---

[28] For the uninitiated, the dog algae poisoning topic is real. See Christine Hauser, "Algae Can Poison Your Dog," *The New York Times* (August 12, 2019). www.nytimes.com/2019/08/12/us/blue-green-algae-dogs.html.

[29] We were additionally interested to understand what psychological considerations motivate people to join issue publics. Hence, in Wave 1 of the MTurk study, we asked respondents (those who said they care about an issue) an additional open-ended question: "In a sentence or two, why do you care about that issue?" We inspected these responses and coded them according to whether the respondent mentioned being personally affected by the issue or not. We found that 15.9 percent of issue public members explicitly mention having a personal stake in the issue they mentioned. (Example response: "As a [marijuana] user, I would like to see the laws changed on this issue so that I can continue to use without fear of loosing [sic.] my job or family.") However, we also note that this is likely an underestimate. There were many close calls, and we suspect that several respondents had a personal stake in the issue, but did not describe it specifically enough to activate our coding. (Example response from a respondent who said they care about women's rights: "It is close to my heart. Women deserve the same respect men do.") We recommend future studies develop approaches to identify personal stakes in more detail.

Table 4 Examples of specific policies respondents mention

Health care gaining a cure diseases such as cancer, Alzheimer, etc.
Childcare
Animal rights and rescue
Antisemitism
*The huge discrepancy in which men are awarded child custody in the family
    court system*
Child trafficking
Lowering the age of Medcare/aid
ending the fillabuster [sic.]
Type one diabetes
*The fact that, with the homelessness issue, most homeless people want to remain
    on the streets*
Repair the nations [sic.] infrastructure
People without kids not able to get Medicare
I care about monetary policy in the Fed
algae dog poisoning
I care about how healthcare workers abuse the elderly in retirement homes
Bounties on soldiers heads that Trump did nothing about
All issues relating to seniors, poverty and hunger
*I took two jobs to pay for college so not happy with those who took out loans get
    bailed out*
Tax religious figures and put tighter restrictions on religion
*Getting my military retirement pay reduced thanks to being 40% disabled. It
    should not be reduced as I earned it while on active duty*

Note: The table shows selected verbatim responses to the open-ended issue public
question, in the PFUNC dataset.

Issue publics potentially have a role to play in such accounts, since they
represent a force that, at least episodically, could ameliorate such stratification.
Even if (for instance) knowledgeable people are *generally* more participatory
and influential, issue publics might represent a route for unknowledgeable
people to exert domain-specific influence in areas that are particularly significant to them. For these reasons, we are interested to explore how issue public
membership relates to widely accepted correlates of political involvement.
While we are not prepared to offer a full account of how extensively issue
publics adjust the accepted contours of political engagement, we can begin to
assess their potential for doing so.

Wave 1 of our MTurk instrument measured two personal traits that are
associated with political influence: interest in politics, and political knowledge.

Interest was measured with a standard question that routinely appears on the ANES: "Some people seem to follow what's going on in government and public affairs most of the time – whether there's an election going on, or not. Others aren't that interested. How much would you say you follow what's going on in politics?" Political knowledge was measured with a four-question battery on current topics.[30]

As we have described, the PFUNC dataset is larger and more diverse. However, because our space on the instrument was limited, we are reliant on items added by other investigators, with other purposes in mind. Still, there were three measures that we thought would help us understand what kinds of people join issue publics. The first is a standard measure of party identification – the formulation that routinely appears on the ANES. This measure allows us to examine whether independents or partisan voters are more likely to join issues publics. Second is a six-item question assessing ideological self-placement, which allows us to assess whether ideological extremists are more likely to join issue publics.[31] Respondents were asked, "In general, do you think of yourself as . . .," with the response options "very liberal," "liberal," "moderate, middle of the road," "conservative," "very conservative," or "I haven't thought about much this." We fold this measure about its midpoint to create a summary measure of ideological extremity.

Third, PFUNC measured respondents' positive or negative feelings toward the Democratic and Republican Parties, using an approach called a "feeling thermometer." In a feeling thermometer, respondents assign a score from 0 to 100 to each of the two parties, with higher numbers indicating that the respondent has more favorable feelings toward that party. We calculate the difference between these two scores, and then take the absolute value of the resulting number. Doing so generates a measure of "affective polarization" – a strong indicator of a hostile orientation to the political sphere (Iyengar et al. 2019). For analysis, we divide this measure into five approximately equally sized bins, ranging from very low to very high affective polarization.

---

[30] We are aware of spirited discussions about trade-offs between various approaches to measuring political knowledge (e.g. Barabas et al. 2014). Our four questions focused on "surveillance" knowledge about current events, but future work could consider measuring other kinds of knowledge. The four questions were: (1) Do you happen to know who is currently Donald Trump's Chief of Staff? [John F. Kelly]; (2) Do you happen to know who was the Chair of Hillary Clinton's presidential campaign? [John Podesta]; (3) Do you happen to know the name of a person that Barack Obama nominated to be a Supreme Court justice, but who was never confirmed by the Senate? [Merrick Garland]; (4) Do you happen to know what public office Steven Mnuchin currently holds? [Secretary of the Treasury]. The scale derived from these measures is reliable (Cronbach's alpha = 0.78).

[31] Of course, we are referring to ideological extremism in the symbolic, not the operational sense (see Ellis & Stimson 2012 on this distinction).

Table 5 reports how common issue public membership is, for different levels of these measures. For each level, we report the proportion of respondents who both (1) said that there was a specific issue they cared about and (2) were able to articulate in a way that our coder could understand. It bears emphasis that these proportions are conservative – for instance since survey fatigue could lead someone not to describe an issue they care about, even if they have one.

There are too few respondents at the lowest levels of political interest to say anything conclusive about their likelihood of joining issue publics. However, it is noteworthy that, of the eighty-three respondents at the middle level of political interest, 63 percent mentioned a codable political issue – initial evidence that issue attention reaches down below the highest levels of political engagement. Performance across our political knowledge measure has a more even distribution. Here, too, we see evidence that it is not only the most politically attentive citizens who can articulate an issue they care about: even among the seventy-eight respondents who answered all of our political knowledge questions incorrectly, 65 percent were able to specify a specific issue that they care about.

The correspondence with partisanship is also fairly weak: the highest rate of issue public membership comes from independents who lean toward one party – a departure from the tendency for strong partisans to be more politically engaged. For both ideology and affective polarization, the relationship runs in the direction one might expect: strong ideologues and people who are more polarized are more likely to identify an issue they care about. Still, the trend is moderate. Thirty-two percent of ideological moderates and 25 percent of people at the lowest level of affective polarization described an issue they care about.

These results increase our confidence that issue publics have the potential to shape the contours of political involvement.

Do Issue Publics Endure Over Time?

An obvious concern about most efforts to assess interest in specific political issues – and ours is no exception – is that they could be epiphenomenal. In particular, when people say they care about an issue, they might simply be reporting – with or without knowing it – issues that are salient, because they recently received significant media attention. In this case, the results throughout this section (particularly Table 2) might substantially overstate the case. Perhaps most of these respondents can think of an issue they heard about recently, but this is does not have any particular long-run psychological influence.

Table 5 Interest, knowledge, and issue public membership

	MTurk		
Follow politics?	**Proportion Issue Public**	**PK (Questions correct)**	**Proportion Issue Public**
Hardly at all (*N* = 6)	0.33	None (*N* = 78)	0.65
Only now and then (*N* = 9)	0.44	One (*N* = 49)	0.76
Some of the time (*N* = 83)	0.63	Two (*N* = 39)	0.82
Most of the time (*N* = 105)	0.84	Three (*N* = 53)	0.87
All of the time (*N* = 62)	0.84	All (*N* = 48)	0.90
	PFUNC		
Partisanship		**Ideology**	
Pure independent (*N* = 244)	0.30	Haven't thought about (*N* = 208)	0.14
Independent leaner (*N* = 320)	0.45	"Middle of the road" (*N* = 825)	0.32
Not strong partisan (*N* = 534)	0.32	Weak ideologues (*N* = 851)	0.38
Strong partisan (*N* = 1,046)	0.38	Strong ideologues (*N* = 523)	0.47
Affective polarization			
Very low (*N* = 472)	0.25		
Low (*N* = 482)	0.34		
Moderate (*N* = 467)	0.34		
High (*N* = 496)	0.42		
Very high (*N* = 490)	0.42		

One way to assess the durability of issue public membership is to examine over-time reliability: Do individuals stipulate the same issue to be personally important when reinterviewed after a delay? To assess over-time reliability of issues captured by our open-ended measure, all of our Wave 2 instruments (and our Wave 3 MTurk instrument) repeated the core issue public questions asked in

Table 6 Reliability of open-ended issue public measure

	MTurk		
	W2 same as W1 (%)	W3 same as W1 (%)	All three the same (%)
Proportion	63.5	57.4	50.0
Analytical N	170	148	138
	PFUNC		
Proportion	33.9	–	–
Analytical N	257	–	–

Note: The analytical N is the number of respondents who were classified as issue public members in Wave 1, and who also completed the subsequent (e.g. Wave 2) instrument.

the earlier wave. As Table 1 shows, the time lags here are considerable: about three months in the PFUNC study, and up to five months in the MTurk study.

We coded the responses to the open-ended question, assessing whether or not the respondent referred to the same issue, upon reinterview. To the extent participants reported the same issue to be personally important after a lag, it suggests durability: the same issues come to mind as personally important, even as circumstances change.[32] Changes over time, on the other hand, are difficult to interpret. To be sure, some such changes imply that the initial response was epiphenomenal. But others could simply mean that the respondent has more than one personally important issue, and they happened to choose the other one when reinterviewed. Or, particularly in the PFUNC study, respondents could simply have been weary of the survey and disinclined to spend time answering an open-ended survey question. (Because this study had material for several different research projects, the instrument was lengthy.) For this reason, we believe this approach, like others reviewed in Section 2, leads to a conservative measure of issue public membership.

Table 6 reports the results of this analysis. The MTurk results are propitious for the open-ended approach. Even after a delay of five months, 57.4 percent of respondents state – with no cues – the same issue to be personally important. Half of respondents mention the same issue in all three waves – a high bar. Over-time reliability is substantially lower in the PFUNC study. But, especially

---

[32] And the circumstances changed markedly. The five-month interval of our MTurk study included a midterm federal election that shifted partisan control of the House of Representatives, for instance. The timeframe for the PFUNC study coincided with early months of the Biden administration, especially its push to vaccinate Americans against Covid-19.

given the overall lower level of attentiveness in this study, it is high enough that we remain confident that a considerable proportion of issues named in response to the open-ended prompt reflect genuine, long-standing issue commitments.[33]

How Well Do Closed-Ended Items Reveal Personally Important Issues?

As we review in Section 3, the most common survey-based approach for identifying issue publics is to ask closed-ended, issue-specific importance questions. We wanted to compare our open-ended item to the standing approach, to develop a sense of how they coincide. We did so in a few different ways.

First, immediately after participants used the open-ended response to report their personally important issue, we asked them "How important is this issue to you personally?" with the standard five response options. Due to space limitations, we asked this question on Wave 1 on the MTurk study only, though we asked similar questions on Wave 2 of both studies, as described next. The question provides a contemporaneous measure of how the issue mentioned in open-ended format registers on the standard closed-ended measure.

While useful, this item only gets us so far. It would be helpful if we also could compare the issue pulled from a respondent's open-ended response to *other* issues in a principled way. Our studies included a more elaborate procedure designed to accomplish this. For exposition, we describe the procedure as it unfolded in the MTurk study, and then note a few modifications we applied to the PFUNC study.

After participants specified their personally important issue, we presented them with a battery of several other issues – the fifteen listed in Table 3. And we provided respondents with the following instructions:

> Next, we'd like to get a sense of how much you care about various issues in politics. Below is a list of fifteen political issues. Please put the issues in order from the one you care about the most (at the top) to the one you care about the least (at the bottom). To move an item up or down in the list, click on it and then click the up or down arrows. Please do not worry too much about the exact position of any particular item. We simply would like a general sense of which issues you care about most and least.

The aim of this exercise was to identify which issues, out of a wide array that covers many facets of politics, respondents regard as more and less important.[34]

---

[33] One hint that this statistic is deflated by rushed survey responding is that, of the 257 individuals in this analysis, 78 (30.4 percent) answered "No" to the first issue public question and thus did not need to enter an open-ended response at all. Of respondents who entered open-ended responses, 48.6 percent mentioned the same issue that they mentioned in Wave 1.

[34] A potential concern about this measure is satisficing. Dragging fifteen issues into a particular order is a fairly onerous task – one that respondents might do in a halfhearted way, or not at all.

From the full ranking, we flagged each respondent's first-ranked issue, their seventh-ranked issue, and their fifteenth-ranked issue for extra scrutiny. These issues represent ones that, in comparison to a long menu of other options, subjects regard as high, medium, and low importance.[35] Thus, we have four issues for comparison: an issue public issue (from the open-ended question), and three issues ranked as high, medium, and low importance.

During the interval between Waves 1 and 2, a coder read all the open-ended issue importance questions that participants wrote, and, if a specific issue could be gleaned from them, came up with a short label for the issue. For instance, one respondent wrote that he or she cared about "entitlement spending and welfare payments," which we labeled, "Welfare Policy." Another wrote about "[p]ublic transportation and passenger train service," which we labeled, "Infrastructure." Then, in Wave 2, respondents were presented with the closed-ended personal importance question once more. This time, we programmed the software to preload labels of four key issues: the issue public issue, plus three (high, medium, and low importance) pulled from the ranking exercise.

The procedure on the PFUNC study was similar, with the following differences. First, due to space constraints, the ranking exercise occurred on Wave 2, rather than Wave 1. We expect this approach to make the closed-ended importance items perform better, since the closed-ended items will be based on a ranking that just occurred. Second, the PFUNC list also included the respondent's issue public issue (from Wave 1), if there was one we could successfully code. If the respondent ranked this issue in one of the critical spots (first, seventh, or last), we chose an adjacent issue for a comparison point in what comes next.[36] Third, since we included the respondent's issue public issue on the list, it expanded to sixteen issues total, and we made appropriate adjustments

---

Thus, the starting order of the issues was randomized, ensuring that no issue was systematically advantaged by its ordering.

[35] We run into a problem if the issue that a person provided in his or her open-ended response is one of the issues in our array of fifteen, and is ranked in one of the critical spots (first, seventh, or fifteenth). In this case, we cannot compare the issue public issue to a first-ranked issue (for instance), since they are the same thing. When such conflicts arise, we substitute the adjacent-ranked issue: we substitute the second-ranked issue for the first, the sixth-ranked issue for the seventh, and the second-to-last ranked issue for the last.

[36] We run into yet another challenge if the respondent's issue public issue from Wave 1 happened to be one of the issues on our list of fifteen. (E.g. the respondent, unprompted, volunteered abortion policy as the issue they cared about.) Without providing for this contingency, the abortion issue would appear twice in the ranking task. Thus, when a respondent happened to choose one of our stipulated issues as their issue public issue, we kept the number of issues constant by subbing in a "backup" issue that nobody volunteered ("automobile registration fees").

Table 7 Responses to closed-ended personal importance question

	MTurk				
	IP Issue (W1) (%)	IP Issue (W2) (%)	#1 Issue (W2) (%)	#7 Issue (W2) (%)	#15 Issue (W2) (%)
Not at all	0.0	0.6	8.6	8.0	11.0
Slightly	1.5	2.5	22.1	20.4	23.3
Moderately	7.0	8.0	28.2	31.5	31.9
Much	33.0	13.5	16.0	19.1	20.3
Very much[37]	58.5	75.5	25.2	21.0	13.5
Total	100.0	100.0	100.0	100.0	100.0
Mean:	3.49	3.61	2.27	2.25	2.02
N	200	163	163	162	163

	PFUNC			
	IP Issue (W2) (%)	#1 Issue (W2) (%)	#7 Issue (W2) (%)	#16 Issue (W2) (%)
Not at all	4.5	9.7	13.0	24.0
Slightly	7.7	7.7	11.4	16.3
Moderately	13.4	13.8	30.9	23.2
Much	14.2	17.4	17.1	17.1
Very much	60.3	51.4	27.6	19.5
Mean:	3.18	2.93	2.35	1.92
N	247	247	246	246

Note: The table shows the distribution of answers to the closed-ended personal importance item, for respondents' open-ended issue public issue, as well as points of comparison from the issue ranking measure.

(e.g. editing the instructions and choosing the sixteenth, rather than fifteenth, to represent a low-importance issue).

Table 7 reports the distribution of answers to this question. Several results bear discussion. First, the issue public issue stands out as being highly important. On the MTurk study, it is more than one point more important (on a five-point scale) than the issue the respondent stipulates to be the most important out of fifteen. This is true whether we consider the issue public issue as represented on Wave 1

---

[37] These are the response options for Wave 2. The fourth and fifth response options in Wave 1 were slightly different. They were "Very" and "Extremely." In fact, we prefer the Wave 1 options for this question, but the slate listed Table 2 were needed for parallelism with other attitude intensity measures included for exploratory purposes in Wave 2.

or Wave 2. The distance among issues ranked as most and least important, in contrast, is comparatively small – the #1 and #7 issues are rated almost identically, and even the #15 issue is only 0.25 points lower. Second, the issue public issue is rated approximately the same in Waves 1 and Wave 2. The correlation between Wave 1 and Wave 2 evaluation is 0.31.[38]

The basic pattern as exhibited on the PFUNC study is similar, though the contrasts are somewhat less stark. The issue public issue "beats out" even the top-ranked issue, even though it was reported several weeks earlier and the ranking exercise was, in this study, completed a few moments earlier. The relevant difference is smaller in magnitude, but still statistically significant (two-tailed $p < 0.01$). As is natural, the middle- and low-ranked issues register as less important on the closed-ended item.

Table 6 also illustrates another apparent deficiency in the closed-ended measure: They lead to false positives, in the sense that a substantial proportion of respondents indicated that their lowest-ranked issue is quite important to them. Perhaps these individuals mean to indicate that the lowest-ranked issue is important in some abstract sense, or perhaps they are reluctant to admit not caring about *any* political issue. But the broader point is that, in this test, the closed-ended item provides poor guidance about which issues are more important than others.

Table 6 also contains a hint that the closed-ended item could lead to false negatives. For instance, in Wave 1, 41.5 percent of respondents indicated that their issue public issue was less than "extremely" important to them. These responses might be sincere. For instance, perhaps these respondents do not care about any political issue – even the one captured in by the open-ended measure, very much. But it is important to remember that *relative* importance could matter here. The issue public issue might still be particularly influential, since it is more important *than others*. But the familiar approach might not reveal as much

A Further Test of Relative Importance and Durability

The ranking task we have described in this section provides an additional way to assess whether the issues respondents provided in response to our open-ended measure are durably perceived as more important than others. All of our follow-up surveys (MTurk Wave 2, MTurk Wave 3, and PFUNC Wave 2) included a version of the issue ranking task. In each of these tasks, we included the issue public

---

[38] We strongly suspect that the change in response options discussed in the previous footnote deflated this correlation. When we examine movement going from Wave 2 to Wave 3 (wherein the response options stayed the same), the correlation is $r = 0.66$.

Table 8 Even after a lag, respondents rank their issue public issue above others

	MTurk Wave 2	MTurk Wave 3	PFUNC Wave 2
Respondents' issue public issue ranking (median)	2	2	2
Highest median among remaining fifteen issues	5	4	5
Next-highest-ranked issue	Health-care policy and gun control (tie)	Health care	Health-care policy and coronavirus (tie)

Note: Analysis is limited to respondents who provided a codable issue public issue in Wave 1.

issue (from Wave 1) amidst the other issues (in a randomly assigned initial position). We were interested in whether participants, unprompted, would rank the issue public issue above the others. This is a demanding test, since placing the issue public issue in a high position requires respondents to recognize what they wrote several weeks earlier, and then rank it higher than a compelling set of alternatives (Table 3).

By and large, respondents passed the test. As Table 8 shows, the median respondent placed the issue public issue in the second spot, out of fifteen. In contrast, the next highest-ranked issue on the list – health-care policy, sometimes tied with another issue – had a median rank of four or five. This is evidence that the typical issue public member durably sees their issue public issue as more important than most focal issues of the day.

Conclusion

In this section, we have presented evidence from two studies conducted two years apart that significant proportions of Americans can name a political issue that they care about more than others. Moreover, we have shown that these perceptions are fairly durable, and that they are more likely to isolate specific issue public issues than approaches that rely on a prespecified list of issues.

One thing we have not done, however, is directly assess the potential of issue public attitudes to directly influence important political judgments. We take up that question in our final empirical section.

5 Voting on Issues

Although the results presented in the previous section show that many Americans have an issue that they persistently think of as being more long-run important than others – one that other measurement approaches might easily miss – we have not yet developed a case that they are politically consequential – the third part of the definition we lay out in Section 3. It might be the case that issue public attitudes really exist, but they are consistently overwhelmed by other political considerations that come to mind – candidate traits, performance evaluations, identities, for some highlighted in the public opinion literature – meaning they exert little influence on political judgments. Unfortunately, the *particularistic* nature of issue public membership – issue publics are numerous, and their memberships are often small – presents a serious measurement challenge. How can researchers design a survey instrument that gives all issue attachments an opportunity to demonstrate their significance, when the relevant issues are not known until respondents tell the researchers what they are?

Our answer to this challenge is inspired by a classic public opinion study. Sullivan et al. (1979) sought to examine whether Americans were becoming more politically tolerant over time. The problem they confronted was that tolerance is only a meaningful concept when it is connected to a person or group that someone dislikes. (Anyone can "tolerate" a group that they like.) And, the set of groups that people liked and disliked itself evolved over time: where it was fashionable to hate atheists in the 1950s, American antipathy had shifted toward communists and racists by the 1970s.

Sullivan, Piereson, and Marcus addressed this difficulty with a two-step approach. First, they asked survey respondents to identify the political group that they liked the least. Respondents did this by choosing a group from a list provided by the researchers, or they could name their own group. Next, the researchers asked the respondents a series of questions evaluating each respondent's willingness to censor and discriminate against whatever group they named. In this way, the researchers devised a "content-controlled" survey measure that assessed tolerance of each respondent's least-liked group – whatever group that happened to be.

Our approach adapts the basic logic of a content-controlled survey measure to the study of issue publics. We incorporate content-controlled elements into a conjoint experiment (Hainmueller & Hopkins 2015) – a popular experimental approach suited to compare the weight that various considerations carry when people make a choice, such as about whom to vote for. Because the essence of our approach is to present each survey respondent with a conjoint experiment tailored specifically for them, we call it a "bespoke" conjoint experiment.

The bespoke conjoint experiment was embedded in our follow-up surveys (MTurk Waves 2 and 3, and PFUNC Wave 2). Immediately after the open-ended issue public question in these waves, participants were told:

> On the next ten [PFUNC: five] screens, we will ask you to consider hypothetical candidates who could run for Congress. We are asking that you consider candidates who could run in a [Party] primary election, so all of the candidates you will evaluate are [Party]. You will see biographical information about each candidate, as well as some information about the stances each has taken on various political issues. Please press the ≫ button when you are ready to continue.

For the [Party] placeholders, the survey software filled in the political party that the respondent said he or she identified with.[39] Thus, we simulated a primary election for the respondent's own political party. We chose to focus on primary elections because we thought issue-based considerations would likely be more influential in a circumstance that put partisan cues in the background. Moreover, primary elections are (one of us is wont to preach) a critical institutional feature of the American political system. As Donald Trump's hostile takeover of the Republican Party in 2016 clearly illustrates, primary elections are where competition among candidates forges the party's identity, its messaging, and its priorities. Additionally, they appear to be an important contributor to the political polarization that currently afflicts American politics (e.g. Kujala 2020). This said, in other studies, we find that issue-based attitudes influence political judgments even when party cues are present (Ehlinger 2019).

In the conjoint experiment, respondents viewed ten (MTurk) or five (PFUNC) pairs of political candidates. Each candidate had five biographical details, listed in a random order: religion; sex; veteran status; age; and former occupation. (Appendix B lists what levels each of these details could take.) Additionally, the conjoint instrument described four policy stances for each candidate (also listed in a random order). The first three related to each of the high-, medium-, and low-importance issues, as defined by the ranking task described in Section 4. In the MTurk study, this issue ranking task took place in Wave 1, and responses drawn from it were piped into conjoint experiments conducted in Waves 2 and 3.[40] In the PFUNC study, space limitations prevented us from including the ranking task in Wave 1. So, we included the ranking task

---

[39] For the MTurk study, this information was piped in from the respondent's Wave 1 response. For PFUNC, it was based on a standard party identification question placed earlier in the questionnaire.

[40] The ranking task was nevertheless repeated in Waves 2 and 3 of MTurk, as described in Chapter 4. However, only the Wave 1 ranking answers were ever used to populate the conjoint experiments.

in Wave 2 and programmed logic to include each respondent's high-, medium-, and low-ranked issue in the conjoint experiment occurring just a few moments later. This attribute will be relevant to interpreting our results: the PFUNC study will compare the respondent's issue public issues (measured months earlier) to issues that the respondent *currently* stipulates to be important. The MTurk study will examine several issues' relative decay in influence over time.

The fourth policy was a stance for the respondent's own issue public issue (defined by their open-ended response in Wave 1). This is the "bespoke" part of the design: each respondent considered candidate stances on whatever issue they had, a few weeks earlier, named in response to our open-ended question.[41] Our process for devising these policy stances bears some elaboration, as it is one of the most labor-intensive and distinctive parts of our research.

While we could write issue stances for the fifteen issues listed in Table 3 in advance, there was no way to know ex ante which issues participants would stipulate to be personally important issues. Therefore, we had a rigid time frame – the interval between Waves 1 and 2, which was as short as three weeks (Table 1) – during which to code the topics that came up in participants' issue public responses, and write a specific policy item related to each. For the MTurk study, we wrote fifty-one specific policies. For PFUNC, we wrote sixty-eight, many of which applied to single survey respondents.

Figure 5 shows a sample judgment task. This figure shows how the conjoint might have looked to a hypothetical respondent who stipulated student loan relief to be their issue public issue in Wave 1, and who stipulated marijuana policy, immigration policy, and genetically modified organisms to be their high-, medium-, and low-importance issues in the ranking task. The policy associated with the student loan issue – "Relief for Americans with student loan debt from the federal government" – is one of the policy stances we wrote between Wave 1 and Wave 2.

After the respondent completed the conjoint task, the instrument presented the four policy stances once more and asked whether the respondent him or herself supported or opposed each. This crucial step was to ensure that we would correctly code the imaginary candidates' stances as being ones that the respondent would like or dislike.[42] Candidates were coded as being *consistent* with the respondent on a given issue when the candidate

---

[41] This property distinguishes our study from another recent conjoint experiment that examined issue voting. Leeper & Robison (2020) measure issue importance, but they do so using the closed-ended measures we critique in Chapter 3, and they do so only for a stable list of five issues.

[42] Alternatively, we could have assumed that the respondent had policy stances typical of his or her political party, but this would be a tenuous assumption, especially given that part of our purpose in this broader project is to assess whether issue opinions can cause deviation from standard party voting.

Candidate Attributes

	Candidate A	Candidate B
Former Occupation	Business	Business
Age	72	71
Religion	Presbyterian	Jewish
Sex	Male	Female
Veteran Status	Served	Did not serve

Candidate Policies

	Candidate A	Candidate B
Increasing restrictions on genetically modified organisms.	Supports the policy	Supports the policy
Relief for Americans with student loan debt from the federal government.	Candidate has not taken a position on this issue	Opposes the policy
Preserving marijuana's status as a schedule I drug per the Controlled Substances Act.	Candidate has not taken a position on this issue	Opposes the policy
Increased restrictions on legal immigration to the United States.	Candidate has not taken a position on this issue	Opposes the policy

Please indicate below whether you would rather vote for candidate A or B.

Candidate A	Candidate B

Figure 5 Conjoint experiment

Note: Example bespoke conjoint judgment task. In this example, the respondent ranked marijuana policy as his or her most important issue, immigration policy as seventh-most important, and regulations on GMOs as the fifteenth-most important. Student loan relief was this respondent's issue public issue.

supported a policy that the respondent favored. Candidates were coded as *inconsistent* with the respondent if they opposed a policy that the respondent favored. If respondents reported a neutral stance or the candidate's policy position was not revealed, the candidate's position was coded as *neither consistent nor inconsistent*.

The main results of the bespoke conjoint experiment are displayed in Figure 6. Here, we include only respondents who were coded as belonging to some issue public. And for parsimony, we focus only on issue positions. Results that include the effects of biographical information are available in Appendix E, Figure E1. The estimates are represented as average marginal component effects (AMCEs), which are standard for similar conjoint designs (Hainmueller et al. 2014). Formally, AMCEs are the marginal effect of a given candidate attribute on a respondent's vote choice over the joint distribution of all other candidate attribute combinations. In substantive terms, the coefficient can be understood as change in the probability of a candidate being selected as they move from the baseline on a given attribute to a different attribute level. For example, the coefficient of 0.122 corresponding to the top point estimate in the left panel of Figure 6 illustrates a 12.2 percent increase in a candidate being selected when the candidate has a consistent issue public position (i.e. when the hypothetical candidate's position aligns with the respondent's issue preferences) relative to when the candidate is neither consistent nor inconsistent (the excluded reference category).

The left panel of Figure 6, focused on MTurk Wave 2, reveals a pronounced effect for a candidate's stance on the issue public issue – both when the issue stance is inconsistent with the respondent's preference and when it is consistent.[43] The effects of all other issues are weaker. For instance, the top-ranked issue has a significant (but smaller) effect on vote choice if the stance is consistent, but no effect when inconsistent. The effects of the seventh- and fifteenth-ranked issues are weaker still. Nearly identical results appear in MTurk Wave 3: even after a delay of several months, respondents recognize and vote on the basis of their issue public issue more than any other issue. In the PFUNC study, displayed on the right, the differences across issues are somewhat more muted. However, recall that the PFUNC test is, in a sense, more demanding. For the MTurk study, issue rankings and the conjoint task were separated by time. For PFUNC, the issue ranking task and the conjoint experiment were presented on the same survey wave, meaning the issue public issue (measured more than three months earlier) was competing with topics pulled from a ranking task presented just moments earlier. Still, as Figure 6 shows, respondents' issue public opinions clearly stand up to opinions on the other topics. And of course the bespoke conjoint approach

---

[43] A programming error in MTurk Wave 2 caused us not to record what policy stances were displayed on the fifteenth-ranked issue for one of the two candidates (the one shown on the right side of each conjoint choice). This error should not bias our estimates: both candidates' stances were randomly assigned and the AMCE estimates derive from variation in stances across many choices. (Having two candidates per screen is not indispensable to the estimation procedure.) However, this does result in slightly more uncertainty about the AMCEs related to the fifteenth-ranked issue in MTurk Wave 2. The authors regret this error.

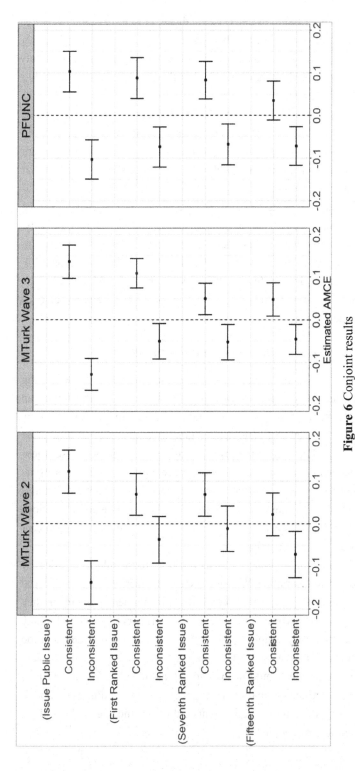

Figure 6 Conjoint results

This figure displays the AMCEs (and associated 95 percent confidence intervals) for the bespoke conjoint task. For each issue, a candidate stance of "neither" is the excluded reference category.

allows a wide variety of issues to enter the candidate policy space that were not included in the ranking exercise either because putting every important issue on the ranking exercise would lead to information overload (e.g. student debt relief) or because the issue would not have occurred to the researchers (e.g. algae dog poisoning, see footnote 28).

Altogether, we see these results as a testament to the potential for issue-based voting, as well as the benefits of measuring issue public membership via an open-ended approach. We must acknowledge that the PFUNC results are somewhat tentative: when the issue public issue competes against issues that were primed earlier in the same survey, it edges out the others by only a small margin. Still, the fact that the issue public issue emerged as the largest influence in three distinct tests increases our confidence in its significance and durability. Thus, issue public attitudes, as captured in our open-ended measure, appear to fulfill our third criterion we laid out in Section 3: they bear on politically significant judgments. In our final section, we step back and consider the evidence we have presented holistically and discuss the role issue preferences play in the broader American political system.

6 The Hidden Significance of Issues

Let us return to the case of Eldon Gould. We started Section 1 by describing Gould's circumstances because his case illustrates the potentially large gap between issue voting as it might exist out in the wild, and the tools that survey researchers use to measure and understand it. Gould, we posit, is part of an issue public. His livelihood hinges on the price of soybeans. He tracks these prices meticulously, receives frequent updates about current events, and discusses the latest developments with friends and associates. Moreover, he readily draws a connection between circumstances that affect his bottom line and the actions of individuals in public office. And, he indicates that he is judging officeholders on the basis of their relevant actions.

Unfortunately, existing approaches in survey research would never identify Gould as an issue public member. We have reviewed dozens of surveys focused on issue voting, and have yet to find one that asks respondents how much they care about the price of soybeans. It is clear why not: survey space is limited, especially for high-quality samples, and soybean farmers simply represent too small a constituency. If a survey were to ask respondents how much they care about soybean prices, why would it not also ask about relief for student loan debt, regulations to protect animal welfare, governmental funding for diabetes research, and any number of other topics that could mean the world – but only to a fairly small number of people?

Scholars' failing to notice and account for any one of these constituencies would be a minor oversight. After all, each is likely to become active and exercise its political influence only in limited circumstances. But we think that the cumulative implication of many such misses is for public opinion researchers to drastically underappreciate the real extent and importance of "issue voting" as a concept. We are reminded of the Paradox of the Heap – a thought experiment where Philosophy students contemplate at what point several individual grains of sand constitute a "heap." Placing one grain of sand on the floor does not make for a heap. Nor does adding a second grain to the first or a third to the second. But with enough grains, a heap will, at some ill-defined point, be present. Because public opinion researchers tend not to notice the individual grains (small issue publics), they could also fail to notice the heap.

The argument we have presented has two main thrusts. First, we present a conceptual critique of how public opinion researchers have sought to measure and assess the prominence issue voting. We argue that existing measures are not well-suited to detect issue publics as they might well exist: as many small, particularistic constituencies. Second, we reinforce this point by showing that, with a revised measurement approach – designed from the ground up to detect particularistic political concerns – issue publics reveal themselves quite readily. Fairly large segments of the population can identify an issue they care about. These concerns endure over time. They come from people who are not otherwise predisposed to participate in politics. And they influence vote choices as much as or more than the focal issues of the day.

A critical take on what we present in this element is that we have not characterized what proportion of the public belongs to issue publics in precise terms. In Table 2, one sample (MTurk) identifies 74.9 percent of respondents as issue public members, but this is in a self-selected group of workers who are rewarded for diligence and attention. The other sample (PFUNC) identifies 35.5 percent, but we see this figure as conservative, for the reasons discussed in Section 4. While we acknowledge this limitation, we also note that addressing it hinges on more than just refined survey procedures – sampling, incentives, attention, and so forth. Citizens' issue commitments undoubtedly vary in their intensity, from people who simply give a particular topic somewhat heightened attention to those who engage in regular sustained activism concerning it. Future attempts to describe the extent of issue public membership should move beyond the somewhat crude binary we indulge here and attempt to describe different degrees of issue public membership. For now, we must settle for rough bounds, while accentuating that even the lower bound represents much more issue-based voting than many researchers would have expected.

An additional critique of our work herein is that our studies go too far in contriving the circumstances most likely to bring issue voting into stark relief. For instance, our conjoint experiment engineers a scenario where two candidates differ on a key issue, even while being identical in terms of the party identification. In the "real world," party identification sends a fairly reliable signal about the slate of policy stances a particular candidate will hold. Citizens largely understand these signals (e.g. Popkin 1991) and will have incorporated their issue positions into their own party identification. The circumstances that generate space between one's own party identification and one's feeling about candidates in a real election will be rare indeed. In short, what we are trumpeting as issue voting might, in the normal course of affairs, quite easily be encompassed by the trusty concept of party identification.

We think this line of critique gives too little attention to V. O. Key's concept of *latent* public opinion (Key 1961, ch. 11). Latent public opinions are those whose effects remain hidden until activated – by a stance, an event, or some other precipitating factor. Key allocates an entire chapter to the idea of latency largely to expound the ways in which latent opinions can constrain elite behavior *even while* they are latent. They would do so through the "rule of anticipated reaction" (263): politicians, having a well-honed sense of how the public *would* react under various hypotheticals, will prospectively take steps to avoid voters' ire. Or, having found themselves in hot water, they will take remedial action as soon as they can. Once again, Eldon Gould's case is illustrative. Recall that just as farmers' support for the Trump administration showed signs of crumbling, the administration spearheaded a multi-billion dollar subsidy program to offset the farmers' economic losses. In essence, the administration paid them off. For our purposes, this episode highlights why it can be essential to construct circumstances that seldom occur. As with a robber's gun that does not go off, *expectations* about what could happen following a misstep are an indispensable strategic factor. We also see an inkling of why politicians find strategic ambiguity about the positions they hold so valuable (e.g. Tomz & Van Houweling 2009).

We believe there is much more to say about the causes and consequences of issue public membership. Here, we have taken issue public membership as a conceptual starting point and had little to say about what factors lead people to join issue publics. This is a promising next direction, especially given our view – discussed in Section 3 – that objective factors such as one's age, gender, or sexuality are of limited utility in predicting what political topics people will care about. One reasonable next step in this vein would be to further scrutinize the ways in which material self-interest is and is not wrapped up in issue public membership (footnote 29, for our first attempt at this question). And although we have examined one obviously important consequence of issue public membership – voting – we have had little to say about consequences for knowledge, attention, cue-taking, emotional arousal, or several other promising topics.

What we have provided, rather, can be understood as a proof of concept – an important one that challenges the prevailing wisdom among public opinion researchers. In a stylized ideal, citizens form opinions about issues of the day and hold politicians accountable for the actions they take on these issues. Among public opinion researchers, subscribing to this ideal – the "folk theory of democracy" – is to risk coming across as a naïve, uninitiated, or unserious. Sustaining it, in one telling, "can now be maintained only by willful denial of a great deal of credible evidence" (Achen & Bartels 2017, 2).

While many critiques of the folk theory are well taken, we think to some degree these critiques are the result of methodologies that do not give the public a fair shake. When researchers employ survey designs that artificially constrain the issue space independently of what the respondent actually cares about (e.g. closed-ended items), it paints a picture of a public whose members often lack sincere issue preferences, much less the ability to hold elites accountable to them. We caution against this interpretation. These conventional designs only demonstrate that respondents fail to hold elites accountable based on issues that *researchers* think are important. This approach is limiting, and it belies the reality that researchers differ from the general population in many politically relevant respects. Furthermore, such designs implicitly require all (or at least many) citizens to hold elites accountable to their preferences on *every* relevant issue. This is an extremely high standard.

A strength of our bespoke conjoint design is that it turns the normal methodologies of issue voting research on their head. We show that when citizens get a chance to tell researchers what matters to them, rather than the other way around, citizens demonstrate more capacity to translate their preferences into political judgment than conventional wisdom would assume. In other words, we need not be experts on everything to hold elites accountable to what really matters to us. In this way, we contend that issue publics may be the overlooked ground where a real form of accountability lives.

We think researchers still need to contend with the possibility that stable, meaningful issue opinions really exist in a modest – but still politically significant – form. Researchers have been slow to come to this realization because of the tools available to them. In concluding, we wish to highlight some of the distinctive procedures we use here and argue that they should play an expanded role in research – on issue publics, but on other topics as well.

The first is our use of open-ended survey items. The linchpin to our effort is a single question where we ask respondents to tell us, in their own words, what political issue they care about more than others. This approach is simple, but uncommon. Landmark surveys such as the ANES or the General Social Survey – and these efforts play a huge agenda-setting role in the discipline – very much favor closed-ended items, where respondents choose which from a manageable set of response options best describes their view. Closed-ended items have some obvious advantages: they impose a lesser burden on the respondent, who does not need to render thoughts into typed sentences. And closed-ended items are much simpler to analyze, since responses come to the researcher in tidy, prepackaged categories.

But the downside of closed-ended items is that the researcher's act of prescribing a limited set of response options sets the agenda in a way that can lead the effort astray. The researcher needs to choose a level of generality that results in a manageable number of categories, and will naturally be inclined to focus on the categories *they* deem plausibly important. In contrast, open-ended items allow the respondent to reveal the associations that occur naturally to them. This complicates the researcher's task: reading several thousand open-ended responses and classifying them as representing a political opinion or not was a labor-intensive part of this project. But as a reward, the researcher gains a clearer view of what is really going on in individuals' heads.[44] We do not expect our open-ended measure will supplant other approaches in all circumstances, but we do hope that other researchers consider it – especially when voters' issue-based attitude intensity is key to project goals.

The second distinctive procedure we invoke here is a "bespoke" experiment, wherein each respondent undergoes a procedure tailored specifically to them. We think of bespoke procedures as a way to cope with a common social scientific problem. Researchers routinely want to study a general concept – in our case, personally important issue opinions – but are confronted with the difficulty that the key construct arises differently among different people. (In our case, everyone's personally important issue is different.) Sometimes the differences are simple enough to address by creating a small number of branched experiments. For instance, a researcher might create parallel experiments about a Democratic- or Republican-endorsed policy, for a study of "partisanship." But as the number of individual categories grows larger, this sort of branching becomes more difficult. We show that the same principle is still possible, even with a fairly large number of categories. Designing such a study is effortful – and it might well require a panel design, so investigators have time to identify the relevant categories and create instrumentation for them – but it can be worth the effort, as it allows one to salvage a general result

---

[44] See Zaller & Feldman (1992) for an overlapping argument.

(personally important issues affect vote choice) in the face of heterogeneous data. One can imagine similar procedures being used to make progress on several other political behavior topics where individual differences create difficulties: identifying the effects of emotionally arousing events in the news; endorsements from admired public figures; or information about how a proposed policy will affect one's own employment sector, for some examples.

Do citizens vote on the issues? It is an important question – one of the "mainline" quandaries to which public opinion researchers have returned over and over, knowing the answer is sure to shape our understanding of peoples' capacity to govern themselves. We undertook this project because the consensus in the field seemed so at odds with what could be readily observed by looking around: people like Eldon Gould, but also citizens who labored to thwart the development of affordable housing (so-called NIMBYs), who halted building new nuclear power plants, who urged employers to adopt transgender-inclusive business practices, and who pointed to Donald Trump's pro-life judicial appointments as a justification for looking past his unseemly behavior. We think the discipline has gone too far in dismissing issue voting as a significant political force. Do citizens vote on the issues? Our answer to the question is yes.

Appendix A

Sample Characteristics

Table A1 Sample characteristics

	MTurk (%)	PFUNC (%)
Race		
White non-Hispanic	–	60.7
Black	–	14.4
Latino	–	17.4
Asian	–	5.9
Other	–	1.5
Education		
No HS diploma	–	2.9
Diploma only	–	40.0
Some college	–	33.4
BA	–	13.7
Graduate degree	–	10.1
Household income		
Under $30,000	–	28.3
$30,000–$49,000	–	19.9
$50,000–$69,000	–	16.7
$70,000–$99,000	–	16.0
$100,000–$149,000	–	11.9
More than $150,000	–	7.2
Age		
18–24	7.2	12.6
25–34	43.8	17.7
35–44	23.6	19.6
45–54	15.4	14.0
55–64	7.2	12.5
65–74	2.4	17.7
75–84	0.0	5.4
85+	0.5	0.6
Sex		
Male	47.6	49.5
Female	52.5	50.3
Other	0.0	0.3

In the MTurk study, age was measured in Wave 2 and sex was measured in Wave 1. In the PFUNC study, all demographics were measured in Wave 1.

Appendix B
Conjoint Attributes and Levels

1) Sex
   a) Male
   b) Female

2) Age
   a) [Uniformly distributed integers from 35 to 75]

3) Religion
   a) Baptist
   b) Catholic
   c) Episcopalian
   d) Jewish
   e) Methodist
   f) Presbyterian

4) Former occupation
   a) Agriculture
   b) Business
   c) Education
   d) Journalism
   e) Law
   f) Medicine
   g) State representative

5) Veteran status
   a) Served
   b) Did not serve

Appendix C
Vote Choice Models

This section presents full results from the regression models discussed in Section 3. Table C1 shows results for Republican primary voters. Table C2 shows results for Democratic primary voters. And Table C3 shows results for the general election. In the Republican primary models, the Party Identification dummies are coarsened, with all Democratic-identifying respondents being lumped into a single category. This is because very few Democratic respondents voted in a Republican primary, and without the coarsening the models are not estimable.

Table C1 Republican primary vote choice models

	(1) Same-sex marriage	(2) Rx drugs	(3) Health insurance	(4) Habeas corpus
Issue opinion	−0.080	0.446	−0.198	0.029
	(0.933)	(1.129)	(2.239)	(1.399)
Issue importance	0.678	0.765	−1.251	0.133
	(0.815)	(0.870)	(1.833)	(0.867)
Opinion × Importance	−0.405	−1.777	−0.290	−0.730
	(1.266)	(1.572)	(2.540)	(1.711)
Pure Independent	−0.497	−0.381	0.164	−0.642
	(1.317)	(1.376)	(1.421)	(1.278)
Leans Republican	−1.663	−1.444	−1.330	−1.753
	(1.182)	(1.201)	(1.255)	(1.119)
Not strong Republican	−0.414	−0.284	−0.276	−0.500
	(1.162)	(1.177)	(1.236)	(1.093)
Strong Republican	−1.371	−1.111	−0.899	−1.303
	(1.137)	(1.159)	(1.218)	(1.079)
Female	0.363	0.345	0.319	0.321
	(0.297)	(0.298)	(0.301)	(0.304)
HS diploma	0.249	0.382	0.125	0.485
	(1.142)	(1.165)	(1.083)	(1.163)
Some college	0.642	0.895	0.506	0.834
	(1.059)	(1.132)	(1.032)	(1.112)

Table C1 (cont.)

	(1) Same-sex marriage	(2) Rx drugs	(3) Health insurance	(4) Habeas corpus
BA	0.288	0.579	0.089	0.480
	(1.125)	(1.148)	(1.051)	(1.145)
Graduate degree	0.423	0.759	0.358	0.652
	(1.132)	(1.174)	(1.084)	(1.165)
Hispanic	0.244	0.279	0.239	0.353
	(0.819)	(0.827)	(0.892)	(0.925)
Other non-Hispanic	0.120	−0.042	−0.252	0.176
	(0.972)	(0.887)	(0.961)	(0.934)
Income	−0.765	−0.644	−0.891	−0.987
	(0.775)	(0.815)	(0.845)	(0.815)
Age	0.721	0.751	0.673	0.701
	(0.787)	(0.761)	(0.821)	(0.786)
Constant	1.044	0.425	2.452	1.332
	(1.536)	(1.690)	(2.020)	(1.613)
Observations	227	228	227	227

Robust standard error in parentheses, ** $p < 0.01$ * $p < 0.05$. A McCain vote is coded as 1 and a Romney vote is coded as 0. There are no Black individuals in these models, so the relevant race coefficient is not estimated.

Table C1 Republican primary vote choice models (continued)

	(5) Wiretap	(6) Work visa	(7) Citizen	(8) Tax >200	(9) Tax <200
Issue opinion	1.572	−2.846	−3.094*	−0.194	−5.020*
	(1.200)	(1.675)	(1.524)	(1.286)	(2.357)
Issue importance	0.868	−3.472*	−1.750	−0.267	−6.949**
	(0.871)	(1.599)	(1.242)	(1.062)	(2.696)
Opinion × Importance	−2.247	3.229	1.987	−1.081	7.269*
	(1.448)	(2.070)	(1.848)	(1.656)	(3.063)
Pure Independent	−0.708	−0.793	−0.369	−0.299	−0.402
	(1.379)	(1.291)	(1.346)	(1.358)	(1.425)
Leans Republican	−1.694	−1.849	−1.912	−1.179	−1.734
	(1.225)	(1.135)	(1.198)	(1.214)	(1.217)
Not strong Republican	−0.419	−0.717	−0.398	−0.112	−0.575
	(1.200)	(1.122)	(1.167)	(1.182)	(1.186)
Strong Republican	−1.311	−1.477	−1.414	−0.843	−1.438
	(1.180)	(1.092)	(1.145)	(1.169)	(1.159)
Female	0.337	0.356	0.092	0.303	0.397
	(0.301)	(0.303)	(0.317)	(0.305)	(0.301)
HS diploma	0.291	0.384	0.166	0.227	0.373
	(1.058)	(1.054)	(1.075)	(1.162)	(1.166)
Some college	0.589	0.875	0.574	0.660	0.568
	(1.012)	(1.012)	(1.031)	(1.124)	(1.102)

Table C1 (cont.)

	(5) Wiretap	(6) Work visa	(7) Citizen	(8) Tax >200	(9) Tax <200
BA	0.252	0.387	−0.115	0.286	0.195
	(1.036)	(1.028)	(1.051)	(1.134)	(1.120)
Graduate degree	0.445	0.491	0.148	0.466	0.437
	(1.053)	(1.045)	(1.077)	(1.164)	(1.140)
Hispanic	0.116	0.305	−0.190	0.619	0.703
	(0.929)	(1.024)	(0.989)	(0.775)	(0.907)
Other non-Hispanic	−0.131	−0.490	−0.481	−0.348	0.084
	(0.936)	(0.881)	(1.013)	(0.975)	(0.888)
Income	−0.997	−1.129	−1.184	−0.309	−1.113
	(0.762)	(0.873)	(0.820)	(0.771)	(0.819)
Age	0.789	0.955	0.991	0.869	0.793
	(0.797)	(0.789)	(0.814)	(0.753)	(0.805)
Constant	0.820	4.224*	4.023*	1.126	6.245*
	(1.542)	(1.713)	(1.640)	(1.588)	(2.492)
Observations	227	228	228	228	227

Robust standard error in parentheses, ** $p < 0.01$ * $p < 0.05$. A McCain vote is coded as 1 and a Romney vote is coded as 0. There are no Black individuals in these models, so the relevant race coefficient is not estimated.

Table C2 Democratic primary vote choice models

	(1) Same-sex marriage	(2) Rx drugs	(3) Health insurance	(4) Habeas corpus
Issue opinion	-1.290*	0.514	1.017	1.823
	(0.576)	(1.214)	(1.010)	(1.186)
Issue importance	-0.060	0.494	0.894	0.952*
	(0.439)	(0.482)	(0.708)	(0.473)
Opinion × Importance	1.025	-1.151	-0.840	-3.069*
	(0.846)	(1.806)	(1.219)	(1.471)
Not strong Democrat	-0.043	-0.090	-0.101	-0.109
	(0.263)	(0.256)	(0.260)	(0.260)
Leans Democrat	-0.257	-0.263	-0.311	-0.337
	(0.302)	(0.308)	(0.308)	(0.303)
Pure Independent	0.241	0.176	0.086	0.188
	(0.439)	(0.429)	(0.428)	(0.434)
Leans Republican	0.640	0.606	0.420	0.595
	(0.622)	(0.566)	(0.607)	(0.591)
Not strong Republican	0.511	0.343	0.187	0.448
	(0.532)	(0.532)	(0.534)	(0.524)
Strong Republican	-0.798	-0.814	-1.032	-0.560
	(0.770)	(0.770)	(0.822)	(0.811)
Female	-0.122	-0.155	-0.144	-0.146
	(0.216)	(0.215)	(0.216)	(0.219)

Table C2 (cont.)

	(1) Same-sex marriage	(2) Rx drugs	(3) Health insurance	(4) Habeas corpus
HS diploma	1.311	1.221	1.271	1.095
	(0.679)	(0.656)	(0.662)	(0.661)
Some college	1.152	1.105	1.095	0.982
	(0.653)	(0.631)	(0.635)	(0.631)
BA	1.879**	1.907**	1.909**	1.734**
	(0.657)	(0.642)	(0.645)	(0.639)
Graduate degree	1.592*	1.686**	1.627*	1.479*
	(0.661)	(0.652)	(0.655)	(0.651)
Black	2.268**	2.151**	2.197**	2.249**
	(0.407)	(0.411)	(0.402)	(0.417)
Hispanic	−0.454	−0.543	−0.534	−0.504
	(0.405)	(0.388)	(0.389)	(0.388)
Other non-Hispanic	−0.659	−0.762	−0.753	−0.840
	(0.595)	(0.605)	(0.607)	(0.620)
Income	−0.299	−0.213	−0.276	−0.240
	(0.509)	(0.510)	(0.519)	(0.508)
Age	−1.487**	−1.586**	−1.651**	−1.641**
	(0.536)	(0.543)	(0.545)	(0.541)
Constant	−0.206	−0.775	−1.168	−0.876
	(0.809)	(0.811)	(0.947)	(0.813)
Observations	478	478	479	478

Robust standard error in parentheses, ** $p < 0.01$ * $p < 0.05$. An Obama vote is coded as 1 and a Clinton vote is coded as 0.

Table C2 Democratic primary vote choice models (continued)

	(5) Wiretap	(6) Work visa	(7) Citizen	(8) Tax >200	(9) Tax <200
Issue opinion	-0.521	-0.775	-0.309	-1.518	-1.208
	(0.906)	(0.869)	(0.934)	(0.800)	(1.191)
Issue importance	0.211	0.333	1.548*	-0.867	-0.736
	(0.479)	(0.688)	(0.629)	(0.506)	(1.249)
Opinion × Importance	0.478	0.909	-0.654	1.717	1.738
	(1.093)	(1.086)	(1.147)	(1.148)	(1.564)
Not strong Democrat	-0.111	-0.161	-0.130	-0.179	-0.100
	(0.257)	(0.256)	(0.261)	(0.259)	(0.258)
Leans Democrat	-0.309	-0.355	-0.358	-0.301	-0.308
	(0.307)	(0.306)	(0.314)	(0.299)	(0.307)
Pure Independent	0.101	0.055	0.050	0.104	0.108
	(0.419)	(0.425)	(0.417)	(0.435)	(0.420)
Leans Republican	0.571	0.412	0.463	0.536	0.485
	(0.586)	(0.593)	(0.564)	(0.590)	(0.573)
Not strong Republican	0.373	0.273	0.344	0.321	0.280
	(0.513)	(0.526)	(0.518)	(0.526)	(0.503)
Strong Republican	-0.812	-1.055	-0.991	-0.906	-0.957
	(0.785)	(0.793)	(0.769)	(0.815)	(0.804)
Female	-0.141	-0.153	-0.183	-0.180	-0.184
	(0.217)	(0.217)	(0.220)	(0.215)	(0.217)

Table C2 (cont.)

	(5) Wiretap	(6) Work visa	(7) Citizen	(8) Tax >200	(9) Tax <200
HS diploma	1.244	1.343*	1.425*	1.318*	1.222
	(0.671)	(0.683)	(0.660)	(0.650)	(0.676)
Some college	1.108	1.195	1.290*	1.167	1.073
	(0.648)	(0.658)	(0.628)	(0.629)	(0.653)
BA	1.896**	2.035**	2.021**	1.914**	1.870**
	(0.658)	(0.670)	(0.634)	(0.637)	(0.663)
Graduate degree	1.644*	1.768**	1.704**	1.669**	1.656*
	(0.665)	(0.675)	(0.639)	(0.648)	(0.672)
Black	2.191**	2.194**	2.244**	2.244**	2.227**
	(0.406)	(0.409)	(0.392)	(0.415)	(0.388)
Hispanic	-0.512	-0.593	-0.897*	-0.496	-0.505
	(0.387)	(0.390)	(0.431)	(0.390)	(0.385)
Other non-Hispanic	-0.791	-0.789	-0.721	-0.797	-0.739
	(0.611)	(0.624)	(0.636)	(0.620)	(0.591)
Income	-0.222	-0.160	-0.359	-0.274	-0.266
	(0.508)	(0.509)	(0.516)	(0.541)	(0.513)
Age	-1.638**	-1.657**	-1.687**	-1.607**	-1.449**
	(0.542)	(0.540)	(0.546)	(0.541)	(0.535)
Constant	-0.509	-0.605	-0.993	0.295	0.014
	(0.829)	(0.903)	(0.872)	(0.813)	(1.105)
Observations	479	478	478	478	478

Robust standard error in parentheses, ** $p < 0.01$ * $p < 0.05$. An Obama vote is coded as 1 and a Clinton vote is coded as 0.

Table C3 Presidential vote choice models

	(1) Same-sex marriage	(2) Rx drugs	(3) Health insurance	(4) Habeas corpus
Issue opinion	1.659**	1.553	1.106	2.597**
	(0.506)	(0.889)	(0.900)	(0.941)
Issue importance	0.908*	0.591	−0.018	0.414
	(0.450)	(0.445)	(0.668)	(0.440)
Opinion × Importance	−0.930	−1.462	−0.026	−1.993
	(0.799)	(1.279)	(1.116)	(1.240)
Not strong Democrat	1.296**	1.366**	1.288**	1.324**
	(0.334)	(0.329)	(0.331)	(0.326)
Leans Democrat	0.861*	0.789*	0.718	0.852*
	(0.380)	(0.385)	(0.379)	(0.377)
Pure Independent	2.548**	2.522**	2.372**	2.556**
	(0.351)	(0.348)	(0.352)	(0.348)
Leans Republican	4.179**	4.186**	3.877**	4.255**
	(0.387)	(0.386)	(0.390)	(0.376)
Not strong Republican	3.749**	3.798**	3.565**	3.803**
	(0.326)	(0.328)	(0.328)	(0.322)
Strong Republican	6.858**	6.902**	6.613**	6.833**
	(0.649)	(0.645)	(0.646)	(0.632)
Female	0.013	−0.065	−0.088	−0.013
	(0.190)	(0.188)	(0.189)	(0.190)

Table C3 (cont.)

	(1) Same-sex marriage	(2) Rx drugs	(3) Health insurance	(4) Habeas corpus
HS diploma	0.070	−0.073	0.093	0.192
	(0.776)	(0.711)	(0.689)	(0.692)
Some college	−0.249	−0.361	−0.313	−0.103
	(0.726)	(0.658)	(0.647)	(0.651)
BA	−0.897	−1.126	−1.152	−0.864
	(0.730)	(0.666)	(0.650)	(0.656)
Graduate degree	−0.599	−0.902	−0.946	−0.493
	(0.739)	(0.671)	(0.653)	(0.660)
Black	−2.696**	−2.444**	−2.527**	−2.445**
	(0.626)	(0.642)	(0.666)	(0.653)
Hispanic	−1.356**	−1.108*	−1.219**	−1.167*
	(0.497)	(0.453)	(0.442)	(0.467)
Other non-Hispanic	−0.976	−0.857	−0.769	−0.771
	(0.647)	(0.639)	(0.683)	(0.673)
Income	0.691	0.371	0.153	0.355
	(0.494)	(0.484)	(0.490)	(0.495)
Age	0.006	0.140	−0.293	0.309
	(0.435)	(0.430)	(0.441)	(0.437)
Constant	−3.401**	−2.710**	−2.222*	−3.188**
	(0.921)	(0.872)	(0.977)	(0.833)
Observations	1,194	1,197	1,197	1,196

Robust standard error in parentheses, ** $p < 0.01$ * $p < 0.05$. A McCain vote is coded as 1 and an Obama vote is coded as 0.

Table C3 Presidential vote choice models (continued)

	(5) Wiretap	(6) Work visa	(7) Citizen	(8) Tax >200	(9) Tax <200
Issue opinion	1.219	2.343*	1.894**	−0.096	2.083
	(0.673)	(0.934)	(0.721)	(0.698)	(1.204)
Issue importance	0.189	1.460	0.536	−1.278*	1.239
	(0.443)	(0.781)	(0.558)	(0.502)	(1.498)
Opinion × Importance	−0.092	−2.033	−1.085	1.733	−1.815
	(0.875)	(1.172)	(0.920)	(0.989)	(1.731)
Not strong Democrat	1.320**	1.270**	1.282**	1.261**	1.311**
	(0.333)	(0.331)	(0.332)	(0.336)	(0.328)
Leans Democrat	0.766*	0.811*	0.679	0.814*	0.761*
	(0.388)	(0.382)	(0.387)	(0.388)	(0.377)
Pure Independent	2.498**	2.475**	2.456**	2.486**	2.524**
	(0.351)	(0.353)	(0.350)	(0.354)	(0.351)
Leans Republican	4.174**	4.232**	4.175**	3.954**	4.190**
	(0.385)	(0.394)	(0.384)	(0.388)	(0.384)
Not strong Republican	3.798**	3.819**	3.747**	3.653**	3.814**
	(0.326)	(0.321)	(0.318)	(0.328)	(0.320)
Strong Republican	6.813**	6.981**	6.899**	6.692**	6.988**
	(0.641)	(0.649)	(0.640)	(0.641)	(0.637)
Female	−0.110	0.019	−0.007	−0.051	−0.098
	(0.193)	(0.190)	(0.190)	(0.190)	(0.188)

Table C3 (cont.)

	(5) Wiretap	(6) Work visa	(7) Citizen	(8) Tax >200	(9) Tax <200
HS diploma	0.066	0.012	0.026	0.018	0.011
	(0.563)	(0.725)	(0.756)	(0.671)	(0.753)
Some college	−0.221	−0.251	−0.296	−0.306	−0.323
	(0.607)	(0.680)	(0.711)	(0.614)	(0.703)
BA	−0.953	−0.933	−0.888	−1.149	−1.052
	(0.610)	(0.684)	(0.714)	(0.620)	(0.706)
Graduate degree	−0.665	−0.666	−0.680	−0.932	−0.835
	(0.613)	(0.685)	(0.717)	(0.621)	(0.707)
Black	−2.364**	−2.455**	−2.514**	−2.736**	−2.410**
	(0.576)	(0.644)	(0.662)	(0.591)	(0.647)
Hispanic	−1.195**	−1.102*	−0.998*	−1.189*	−1.093*
	(0.440)	(0.465)	(0.461)	(0.473)	(0.459)
Other non-Hispanic	−0.841	−0.845	−0.928	−0.797	−0.841
	(0.639)	(0.663)	(0.636)	(0.620)	(0.633)
Income	0.252	0.433	0.582	0.041	0.383
	(0.484)	(0.484)	(0.502)	(0.512)	(0.482)
Age	0.178	0.118	0.080	0.266	0.143
	(0.446)	(0.433)	(0.439)	(0.435)	(0.430)
Constant	−2.739**	−3.939**	−3.322**	−1.491	−3.717**
	(0.829)	(0.960)	(0.905)	(0.851)	(1.391)
Observations	1,197	1,195	1,196	1,197	1,196

Robust standard error in parentheses, ** $p < 0.01$ * $p < 0.05$.

Appendix D

Procedure to Remove Fraudulent Responses from MTurk Study

As noted in the main text, we detected evidence of fraudulent responding in our MTurk study, and took steps to remove fraudulent responses. First, we flagged responses that had either of two features strongly associated with fraudulent responding: (1) their associated IP address appeared more than once in the dataset or (2) they used the word "good" or "nice" in an open-ended response question on the debriefing screen at the end of our study – a pattern that has been linked to fraud in other MTurk samples (Kennedy et al. 2020). Among the flagged observations, we inspected open-ended responses to confirm that we would not be removing a valid response. We would have retained a response if it provided a coherent, context-appropriate answer to any open-ended questions, but there were no such responses. As such, we dropped these observations ($N = 22$) from further participation in the study (Fraud Screen 1).

Not all fraudulent responses have these characteristics, so we looked for signs of problematic responding in the remaining observations – incoherent answers, answers in broken English, or text copy and pasted from elsewhere on the Internet. This scrutiny resulted in an additional thirteen exclusions. Finally, twenty-seven of the remaining responses ceased participation in the instrument before providing information necessary for subsequent waves. Thus, 267 individuals were invited to Waves 2 and 3. Table D1 reports how our analysis sample changed in light of these exclusions.

Table D1 Exclusions applied in Wave 1

Remaining N	Exclusions	Reason
330		Completed Wave 1 Consent
308	22	Failed Fraud Screen 1
294	14	Failed Fraud Screen 2
267	27	Within Wave 1 attrition

Appendix E

Full Conjoint Results

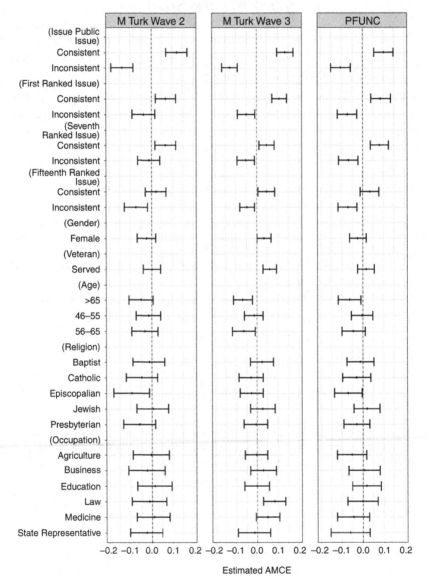

Figure E1 Full conjoint results (all studies)

Note: This figure displays the AMCEs (and associated 95 percent confidence intervals) for the bespoke conjoint task. For each issue, a candidate stance of "neither" is the excluded reference category.

References

Achen, Christopher H., and Larry M. Bartels. 2017. *Democracy for Realists: Why Elections Do Not Produce Responsive Government*. Princeton: Princeton University Press.

Ahler, Douglas J., Carolyn E. Roush, and Gaurav Sood. 2019. "The Micro-Task Market for Lemons: Data Quality on Amazon's Mechanical Turk." *Political Science Research and Methods*: 1–20. www.cambridge.org/core/journals/political-science-research-and-methods/article/abs/microtask-market-for-lemons-data-quality-on-amazons-mechanical-turk/B379D88275 75D81857C872BB5C40B660

Aldrich, John H., John L. Sullivan, and Eugene Borgida. 1989. "Foreign Affairs and Issue Voting: Do Presidential Candidates 'Waltz before a Blind Audience?'" *American Political Science Review* 83(1): 123–41.

Althaus, Scott L. 1998. "Information Effects in Collective Preferences." *American Political Science Review* 92(3): 545–58.

Austen-Smith, David. 1996. "Interest Groups: Money, Information and Influence." In Dennis C. Mueller, ed., *Perspectives on Public Choice*, Cambridge: Cambridge University Press, pp. 296–321.

Barbaro, Michael. 2018. "Pro-Trump, but Fearing His Tariffs." *The New York Times* (April 5). www.nytimes.com/2018/04/05/podcasts/the-daily/us-china-tariffs.html.

Barabas, Jason, Jennifer Jerit, William Pollock, and Carlisle Rainey. 2014. "The Question(S) of Political Knowledge." *American Political Science Review* 108(04): 840–55.

Bartels, Larry. 2000. "Partisanship and Voting Behavior, 1952–1996." *American Journal of Political Science* 44(1): 35–50.

Berinsky, Adam J. 2016. *New Directions in Public Opinion*. New York: Routledge.

Blumer, Herbert. 1948. "Public Opinion and Public Opinion Polling." *American Sociological Review* 13(5): 542–49.

Bolsen, Toby, and Thomas J. Leeper. 2013. "Self-Interest and Attention to News among Issue Publics." *Political Communication* 30(3): 329–48.

Brader, Ted, Joshua A. Tucker, and Dominik Duell. 2013. "Which Parties Can Lead Opinion? Experimental Evidence on Partisan Cue Taking in Multiparty Democracies." *Comparative Political Studies* 46(11): 1485–517.

Bullock, John G. 2011. "Elite Influence on Public Opinion in an Informed Electorate." *American Political Science Review* 105(3): 496–515.

Burns, Nancy, Kay Lehman Schlozman, and Sidney Verba. 2001. *The Private Roots of Public Action*. Cambridge, MA: Harvard University Press.

Campbell, Angus, Philip E. Converse, Warren E Miller, and Donald E Stokes. 1960. *The American Voter*. Chicago, IL: University Of Chicago Press.

Carsey, Thomas M., and Geoffrey C. Layman. 2006. "Changing Sides or Changing Minds? Party Identification and Policy Preferences in the American Electorate." *American Journal of Political Science* 50(2): 464–77.

Chong, Dennis, and James N. Druckman. 2007. "Framing Theory." *Annual Review of Political Science* 10(1): 103–26.

Chyzh, Olga V., and Robert Urbatsch. 2021. "Bean Counters: The Effect of Soy Tariffs on Change in Republican Vote Share between the 2016 and 2018 Elections." *The Journal of Politics* 83(1): 415–19.

Claassen, Ryan L, and Michael J Ensley. 2015. "Motivated Reasoning and Yard-Sign-Stealing Partisans: Mine Is a Likable Rogue, Yours Is a Degenerate Criminal." *Political Behavior* 38(2): 317–35.

Claassen, Ryan L., and Stephen P. Nicholson. 2013. "Extreme Voices." *Public Opinion Quarterly* 77(4): 861–87.

Cohen, Geoffrey L. 2003. "Party over Policy: The Dominating Impact of Group Influence on Political Beliefs." *Journal of Personality and Social Psychology* 85(5): 808–22.

Cohen, Patricia. 2019. "Pain of Tariffs Tests Farmers' Faith in Trump: 'How Long Is Short-Term?'" *New York Times* (May 24). www.nytimes.com/2019/05/24/business/economy/farmers-trump-trade.html.

Converse, Philip E. 1964. "The Nature of Belief Systems in Mass Publics." In David E. Apter, ed., *Ideology and Discontent*, New York: Free Press, pp. 206–61.

1987. "Changing Conceptions of Public Opinion in the Political Process." *Public Opinion Quarterly* 51: S12–24.

Daniels, Jeff and Christina Wilkie. 2019. "Trump Administration Unveils $16 Billion Bailout to Farmers Hurt by China Trade War." *CNBC.com* (May 23). www.cnbc.com/2019/05/23/trump-to-give-16-billion-to-farmers-hurt-by-trade-war-sonny-perdue.html.

Davey, Monica and Patricia Cohen. 2018. "Trade War Prospect Shakes Part of Trump Base: Midwest Farmers." *New York Times*. (March 10). www.nytimes.com/2018/03/10/business/economy/tariffs-farmers.html.

Delli-Carpini, Michael X., and Scott Keeter. 1997. *What Americans Know about Politics and Why It Matters*. New Haven, CT: Yale University Press.

Delton, Andrew W., Peter DeScioli, and Timothy J. Ryan. 2020. "Moral Obstinacy in Political Negotiations." *Political Psychology* 41(1): 3–20.

Druckman, James N. 2001. "On the Limits of Framing Effects: Who Can Frame?" *The Journal of Politics* 63(4): 1041–66.

2004. "Political Preference Formation: Competition, Deliberation, and the (Ir)Relevance of Framing Effects." *American Political Science Review* 98(4): 671–86.

Ehlinger, J. 2019. "That's Where I Draw the Line! How Issue Publics Can Overcome Partisan Tribalism." MA Thesis, University of North Carolina at Chapel Hill.

Ellis, Christopher, and James A Stimson. 2012. *Ideology in America*. New York: Cambridge University Press.

Fenno, Richard E. 1978. *Home Style: House Members in Their Districts*. Boston, MA: Little, Brown.

Feldman, Stanley. 1989. "Measuring Issue Preferences: The Problem of Response Instability." In James A. Stimson, ed., *Political Analysis: An Annual Publication of the Methodology Section of the American Political Science Association*, Vol. 1, Ann Arbor, MI: University of Michigan Press, pp. 25–60.

Fowler, Anthony. 2020. "Partisan Intoxication or Policy Voting?" *Quarterly Journal of Political Science* 15(2): 141–79.

Galston, William A. 2001. "Political Knowledge, Political Engagement, and Civic Education." *Annual Review of Political Science*, Vol. 4, pp. 217–34.

Gershkoff, Amy R. 2006. "How Issue Interest Can Rescue the American Public." Ph.D. Dissertation, Princeton University.

Gilens, Martin. 2001. "Political Ignorance and Collective Policy Preferences." *American Political Science Review* 95(2): 379–96.

2019. "Citizen Competence and Democratic Governance." In Adam Berinsky, ed., *New Directions in Public Opinion*, New York: Routledge, pp. 41–72.

Graham, Matthew H, and Milan W Svolik. 2020. "Democracy in America? Partisanship, Polarization, and the Robustness of Support for Democracy in the United States." *American Political Science Review* 114(2): 392–409.

Green, Donald P., Bradley Palmquist, and Eric Schickler. 2002. *Partisan Hearts and Minds: Political Parties and the Social Identities of Voters*. New Haven, CT: Yale University Press.

Greene, Steven. 1990. "Understanding Party Identification: A Social Identity Approach." *Political Psychology* 20(2): 393–403.

Guntermann, Eric, and Gabriel Lenz. 2022. "Still Not Important Enough? COVID-19 Policy Views and Vote Choice." *Perspectives on Politics* 20 (2): 547–61.

Hainmueller, Jens, and Daniel J. Hopkins. 2015. "The Hidden American Immigration Consensus: A Conjoint Analysis of Attitudes toward

Immigrants: The Hidden American Immigration Consensus." *American Journal of Political Science* 59(3): 529–48.

Hainmueller, Jens, Daniel J. Hopkins, and Teppei Yamamoto. 2014. "Causal Inference in Conjoint Analysis: Understanding Multidimensional Choices via Stated Preference Experiments." *Political Analysis* 22(1): 1–30.

Hall, Richard L., and Alan V. Deardorff. 2006. "Lobbying as Legislative Subsidy." *American Political Science Review* 100(1): 69–84.

Hanretty, Chris, Benjamin E. Lauderdale, and Nick Vivyan. 2020. "A Choice-Based Measure of Issue Importance in the Electorate." *American Journal of Political Science* 64(3): 519–35.

Hauser, David J., and Norbert Schwarz. 2016. "Attentive Turkers: MTurk Participants Perform Better on Online Attention Checks than Do Subject Pool Participants." *Behavior Research Methods* 48(1): 400–07.

Henderson, Michael. 2014. "Issue Publics, Campaigns, and Political Knowledge." *Political Behavior* 36(3): 631–57.

Hillygus, D. Sunshine, and Todd G. Shields. 2008. *The Persuadable Voter: Wedge Issues in Presidential Campaigns*. Princeton, NJ: Princeton University Press.

Hirtzer, Michael. 2019. "Soybeans Slump to Lowest in a Decade as Trade War Intensified." *Bloomberg* (May 13). www.bloomberg.com/news/articles/2019-05-13/grain-soy-soybeans-at-decade-low-amid-trade-war-pig-fever-woes#xj4y7vzkg.

Huddy, Leonie, Lilliana Mason, and Lene Aarøe. 2015. "Expressive Partisanship: Campaign Involvement, Political Emotion, and Partisan Identity." *American Political Science Review* 109(1): 1–17.

Hutchings, Vincent L. 2003. *Public Opinion and Democratic Accountability: How Citizens Learn about Politics*. Princeton, NJ: Princeton University Press.

Iyengar, Shanto. 1990. "Shortcuts to Political Knowledge: The Role of Selective Attention and Accessibility." In John A. Ferejohn, and James H. Kuklinsky, eds., *Information and Democratic Processes*, Urbana, IL: University of Illinois Press, pp. 160–85.

Iyengar, Shanto, Yphtach Lelkes, Matthew Levendusky, Neil Malhotra, and Sean J. Westwood. 2019. "The Origins and Consequences of Affective Polarization in the United States." *Annual Review of Political Science* 22(1): 129–46.

Johns, Robert. 2010. "Measuring Issue Salience in British Elections: Competing Interpretations of 'Most Important Issue.'" *Political Research Quarterly* 63(1): 143–58.

Johnston, Richard. 2006. "Party Identification: Unmoved Mover or Sum of Preferences?" *Annual Review of Political Science* 9: 329–51.

Jones, Jeffrey. 2018. "U.S. Preference for Stricter Gun Laws Highest Since 1993." *Gallup.com.* (March 14). https://news.gallup.com/poll/229562/pref erence-stricter-gun-laws-highest-1993.aspx.

Kam, Cindy D. 2005. "Who Toes the Party Line? Cues, Values, and Individual Differences." *Political Behavior* 27(2): 163–82.

Kennedy, Ryan, Scott Clifford, Tyler Burleigh et al. 2020. "The Shape of and Solutions to the MTurk Quality Crisis." *Political Science Research and Methods* 8(4): 614–29.

Key, V. O. 1961. *Public Opinion and American Democracy.* New York: Knopf.

Kinder, Donald R. 1998. "Opinion and Action in the Realm of Politics." In Daniel Gilbert, Susan Fiske, and G Linzey, eds., *Handbook of Social Psychology,* New York: McGraw-Hill, pp. 778–867.

Kinder, Donald R., and Nathan P. Kalmoe. 2017. *Neither Liberal nor Conservative: Ideological Innocence in the American Public.* Chicago: University of Chicago Press.

Kitroeff, Natalie. 2019. "Caught in the Middle of the Trade War." *The New York Times* (May 16). www.nytimes.com/2019/05/16/podcasts/the-daily/ trump-tariffs-china-trade-war.html?.

Kollman, Ken. 1998. *Outside Lobbying.* Princeton, NJ: Princeton University Press.

Krosnick, Jon A. 1990. "Government Policy and Citizen Passion: A Study of Issue Publics in Contemporary America." *Political Behavior* 12(1): 59–92.

Krupnikov, Yanna, and John Barry Ryan. 2022. *The Other Divide: Polarization and Disengagement in American Politics.* New York: Cambridge University Press.

Kujala, Jordan. 2020. "Donors, Primary Elections, and Polarization in the United States." *American Journal of Political Science* 64(3): 587–602.

Lacombe, Matthew J. 2019. "The Political Weaponization of Gun Owners: The National Rifle Association's Cultivation, Dissemination, and Use of a Group Social Identity." *The Journal of Politics,* pp. 1342–56

Leeper, Thomas J., and Joshua Robison. 2020. "More Important, but for What Exactly? The Insignificant Role of Subjective Issue Importance in Vote Decisions." *Political Behavior* 42(1): 239–59.

Lenz, Gabriel S. 2012. *Follow the Leader?: How Voters Respond to Politicians' Policies and Performance.* Chicago, IL: University of Chicago Press.

Lippman, Walter. 1925. *The Phantom Public.* New Brunswisck, NJ: Transaction Publishers.

Lodge, Milton, and Charles S. Taber. 2013. *The Rationalizing Voter.* New York: Cambridge University Press.

Madson, Gabriel J. 2021. "How Voters Use Issues." Ph.D. Dissertation, Duke University.

Maggiotto, Michael A., and James E. Piereson. 1978. "Issue Publics and Voter Choice." *American Politics Quarterly* 6(4): 407–28.

Markus, Gregory B, and Philip E. Converse. 1979. "A Dynamic Simultaneous Equation Model of Electoral Choice." *American Political Science Review* 73(4): 1055–70.

Mason, Lilliana. 2018. *Uncivil Agreement: How Politics Became Our Identity.* Chicago, IL: University of Chicago Press.

Page, Benjamin I, and Richard A Brody. 1972. "Policy Voting and the Electoral Process: The Vietnam War Issue." *American Political Science Review* 66 (3): 979–95.

Page, Benjamin I, and Robert Y Shapiro. 1992. *The Rational Public*, Chicago: University of Chicago Press.

Pérez, Efrén O. 2015. "Mind the Gap: Why Large Group Deficits in Political Knowledge Emerge – And What to Do about Them." *Political Behavior* 37 (4): 933–54.

Petty, Richard E., and Jon A Krosnick, eds. 1995. *Attitude Strength: Antecedents and Consequences*. Washington, DC: Psychology Press.

Popkin, Samuel L. 1991. *The Reasoning Voter.* Chicago, IL: University of Chicago Press.

Price, Vincent, and John R Zaller. 1993. "Who Gets the News? Alternative Measures of News Reception and Their Implications for Research." *Public Opinion Quarterly* 57(2): 133–64.

Prior, Markus. 2019. *Hooked: How Politics Captures People's Interest.* New York: Cambridge University Press.

Rabinowitz, George, James W. Prothro, and William Jacoby. 1982. "Salience as a Factor in the Impact of Issues on Candidate Evaluation." *The Journal of Politics* 44(1): 41–63.

Rasinski, Kenneth A. 1989. "The Effect of Question Wording on Public Support for Government Spending." *Public Opinion Quarterly* 53(3): 388–94.

Ryan, Timothy J. 2014. "Reconsidering Moral Issues in Politics." *The Journal of Politics* 76(2): 380–97.

2017. "No Compromise: Political Consequences of Moralized Attitudes." *American Journal of Political Science* 61(2): 409–23.

2019. "Actions versus Consequences in Political Arguments: Insights from Moral Psychology." *The Journal of Politics* 81(2): 426–40.

Shapero, Julia. 2022. "Republican Senators Face Pushback from Both Sides on Gun Control." *Axios* (June 19). www.axios.com/2022/06/19/republican-gun-bill-pushback.

Simonovits, Gabor, Jennifer McCoy, and Levente Littvay. 2022. "Democratic Hypocrisy and Out-Group Threat: Explaining Citizen Support for Democratic Erosion." *The Journal of Politics*: 719009.

Sulkin, Tracy. 2005. *Issue Politics in Congress*. New York: Cambridge University Press.

Sullivan, John, James Piereson, and George E. Marcus. 1979. "An Alternative Conceptualization of Political Tolerance: Illusory Increases 1950s–1970s." *American Political Science Review* 73(3): 781–94.

Swanson, Ana. 2018. "Trump to Impose Sweeping Steel and Aluminum Tariffs." *The New York Times* (March 1). www.nytimes.com/2018/03/01/business/trump-tariffs.html.

Taber, Charles S., Damon Cann, and Simona Kucsova. 2009. "The Motivated Processing of Political Arguments." *Political Behavior* 31: 137–55.

Tomz, Michael, and Robert P. Van Houweling. 2009. "The Electoral Implications of Candidate Ambiguity." *American Political Science Review* 103(1): 83–98.

Tourangeau, Roger, and Kenneth A. Rasinski. 1988. "Cognitive Processes Underlying Context Effects in Attitude Measurement." *Psychological Bulletin* 103(3): 299–314.

Verba, Sidney, Kay Lehman Schlozman, and Henry E. Brady. 1995. *Voice and Equality*. Cambridge, MA: Harvard University Press.

Visser, Penny S., George Y. Bizer, and Jon A. Krosnick. 2006. "Exploring the Latent Structure of Strength-Related Attitude Attributes." *Advances in Experimental Social Psychology* 38: 1–67.

Wlezien, Christopher. 2005. "On the Salience of Political Issues: The Problem with 'Most Important Problem'." *Electoral Studies* 24(4): 555–79.

Zaller, John R., and Stanley Feldman. 1992. "A Simple Theory of the Survey Response: Answering Questions versus Revealing Preferences." *American Journal of Political Science* 36(3): 579–616.

Zhang, Bingbing, and Sherice Gearhart. 2020. "Collecting Online Survey Data: A Comparison of Data Quality among a Commercial Panel & MTurk." *Survey Practice* 13(1): 1–10.

Acknowledgments

We received guidance, feedback, and encouragement from numerous individuals while writing this Element. In particular, we would like to thank Alexander Agadjanian, Scott Clifford, Grant Ferguson, and Yphtach Lelkes for reading earlier drafts, as well as our series editor Yanna Krupnikov for shepherding the manuscript through the review process. We are also grateful to two anonymous peer reviewers who provided critical comments that helped us improve the manuscript. We especially thank Marc Hetherington for providing space on the Politics in the Field at UNC survey, as well as for encouragement and advice at every stage of the project. Finally, we wish to express our appreciation to the Department of Political Science at UNC for providing a vibrant and supportive research community. On a personal note, Tim thanks his wife Kathryn, his dog Juniper! (the exclamation point is part of her name), and even the cat Stella. J thanks his fiancé Jennifer and our three adoring cats Charlie, Danny, and Lola.

Cambridge Elements ≡

Political Psychology

Yanna Krupnikov
Stony Brook University

Yanna Krupnikov is Professor of Political Science at Stony Brook University. Her research focuses on political psychology and political communication, and considers when political messages are most likely to affect people's behaviors. Her work with Cambridge University Press include *Independent Politics* (2016, coauthored with Samara Klar), *The Increasing Viability of Good News* (2021, with Stuart Soroka), and *The Other Divide* (2022, with John Barry Ryan).

About the Series

Most political events and outcomes are the results of people's decisions. This series delves into the psychology behind these decisions to understand contemporary politics. The publications in the series explain real-world political events by using psychology to understand people's motivations, beliefs and, ultimately, behaviors.

Cambridge Elements ☰

Political Psychology

Printed in the United States
by Baker & Taylor Publisher Services